CliffsNotes™

The Taming of the Shrew

By Kate Maurer, Ph.D.

IN THIS BOOK

- Learn about the Life and Background of the Author
- Preview an Introduction to the Play
- Study a graphical Character Map
- Explore themes and literary devices in the Critical Commentaries
- Examine in-depth Character Analyses
- Enhance your understanding of the work with Critical Essays
- Reinforce what you learn with CliffsNotes Review
- Find additional information to further your study in CliffsNotes Resource Center and online at www.cliffsnotes.com

WILEY

Wiley Publishing, Inc.

About the Author

Kate Maurer received her Ph.D. in English from Marquette University in 1997. She currently makes her professional home at the University of Minnesota Duluth where she specializes in Shakespeare, New Media, and professional writing in the Fine Arts and Humanities.

Publisher's Acknowledgments

Editorial

Project Editor: Tracy Barr

Acquisitions Editor: Greg Tubach

Glossary Editors: The editors and staff at Webster's New World™ Dictionaries

Editorial Administrator: Michelle Hacker

Composition

Indexer: York Production Services, Inc.

Proofreader: York Production Services, Inc.

Wiley Indianapolis Composition Services

CliffsNotes™ *The Taming of the Shrew*

Published by:
Wiley Publishing, Inc.
111 River Street
Hoboken, NJ 07030
www.wiley.com

Copyright © 2001 Wiley Publishing, Inc., Hoboken, NJ
Library of Congress Control Number: 00-107681
ISBN: 978-0-7645-8673-6
Printed in the United States of America
10 9 8 7 6
1O/TQ/QZ/QW/IN
Published simultaneously in Canada

For general information on our other products and services or to obtain technical support, please contact our Customer Care Department within the U.S. at 800-762-2974, outside the U.S. at 317-572-3993, or fax 317-572-4002.

Wiley also publishes its books in a variety of electronic formats. Some content that appears in print may not be available in electronic books.

Table of Contents

How to Use This Book

This CliffsNotes study guide on Shakespeare's *The Taming of the Shrew* supplements the original literary work, giving you background information about the author, an introduction to the work, a graphical character map, critical commentaries, expanded glossaries, and a comprehensive index, all for you to use as an educational tool that will allow you to better understand *The Taming of the Shrew.* This study guide was written with the assumption that you have read *The Taming of the Shrew.* Reading a literary work doesn't mean that you immediately grasp the major themes and devices used by the author; this study guide will help supplement your reading to be sure you get all you can from Shakespeare's *The Taming of the Shrew.* CliffsNotes Review tests your comprehension of the original text and reinforces learning with questions and answers, practice projects, and more. For further information on Shakespeare and *The Taming of the Shrew,* check out the CliffsNotes Resource Center.

CliffsNotes provides the following icons to highlight essential elements of particular interest:

Reveals the underlying themes in the work.

Helps you to more easily relate to or discover the depth of a character.

Uncovers elements such as setting, atmosphere, mystery, passion, violence, irony, symbolism, tragedy, foreshadowing, and satire.

Enables you to appreciate the nuances of words and phrases.

Don't Miss Our Web Site

Discover classic literature as well as modern-day treasures by visiting the CliffsNotes Web site at www.cliffsnotes.com. You can obtain a quick download of a CliffsNotes title, purchase a title in print form, browse our catalog, or view online samples.

You'll also find interactive tools that are fun and informative, links to interesting Web sites, tips, articles, and additional resources to help you, not only for literature, but for test prep, finance, careers, computers, and the Internet, too. See you at www.cliffsnotes.com!

LIFE AND BACKGROUND OF THE AUTHOR

The following abbreviated biography of Shakespeare's is provided so that you might become more familiar with his life and the historical times that possibly influenced his writing. Read this Life and Background of the Author section and recall it when reading Shakespeare's *The Taming of the Shrew,* thinking of any thematic relationship between Shakespeare's work and his life.

Personal Background

William Shakespeare was born in 1564 in Stratford-upon-Avon, England, northwest of London, to John Shakespeare and Mary Arden. William's father made his living primarily as a tanner and a glover but also traded wool and grain from time to time. John Shakespeare also served in various offices, including high bailiff (like a mayor), the city's highest public office. In the mid-1570s, John Shakespeare's fortune began to decline mysteriously (some say it was because of his wife's Catholicism, although that claim is unsubstantiated), and it was largely mortgages made on properties Mary brought to the marriage that helped to sustain the family.

Although there are no records to prove Shakespeare's enrollment in school, critics accept it with considerable certainty. At school, Shakespeare would have studied reading and writing (in English as well as in Latin), and Greek and Roman writers including Horace, Aesop, Ovid, Virgil, Seneca, and Plautus. The extent to which he would have been familiar with the works of such ancient classics is unknown, but studying Shakespeare's plays and long poems suggests he had at least a degree of knowledge about them in their original forms, not merely translations.

When William Shakespeare was 18, he married Anne Hathaway, 26. Their first child, Susanna, was born the following May; twins, Hamnet and Judith, followed in 1585. Little information is available regarding Shakespeare's life from the time of the twins' birth until 1592. All we know for sure is that by 1592, Shakespeare had arrived in London, leaving his family behind, and had begun what is perhaps the most successful literary career the world has ever known.

Life in London and His Work

In London, Shakespeare was actor and dramatist for The Lord Chamberlain's Men—later renamed The King's Men when James I took the throne in 1603—one of two predominate acting troupes in London at the time (the other was The Lord Admiral's Men, headed by Edward Alleyn with financial banking from Philip Henslowe). In 1599, Shakespeare became a shareholding member of The Lord Chamberlain's Men.

Between the years of 1588 and 1613, Shakespeare wrote 38 plays. His dramatic work is commonly studied in four categories: comedies, histories, tragedies, and romances. In addition, Shakespeare also wrote several Ovidian poems, including *Venus and Adonis* (1593) and *The Rape of Lucrece* (1594). Shakespeare is also well known for his sonnet sequence written in the early 1590s which is comprised of 154 interconnected sonnets dealing with issues such as love, fidelity, mortality, and the artist's power and voice.

The First Folio

Because of the publishing practices of the time and the fact that playwrights, including Shakespeare, didn't write with the intention of preserving their plays but with the goal of making money, it is difficult to pinpoint definitive texts. In Shakespeare's case, only about half of his plays were published during his lifetime. In fact, it wasn't until 1623, seven years after Shakespeare's death in 1616, that all his plays were assembled into one volume. This collection, referred to as *The First Folio* (because it was printed in folio format, the largest, most expensive, and most prestigious kind of book), included previously published plays as well as plays never before published. Some of the works in *The First Folio* can be traced to the author's papers, yet some were re-created from prompt books (annotated play scripts) or even the memories of the actors themselves (helping to explain some of the inconsistencies found in different editions of the plays).

His Reputation as a Playwright

Although we commonly single out Shakespeare's work as extraordinary and deserving of special attention, at the time of the plays' performances, they were typically dismissed as popular entertainment. In fact, Shakespeare was not the most popular dramatist of his time. Ben Jonson, Shakespeare's contemporary (and Britain's first Poet Laureate), and Christopher Marlowe, a slight predecessor to Shakespeare, were both commonly held in higher esteem than the man whose reputation has since eclipsed both of his competitors.

Shakespeare's reputation as Britain's premier dramatist did not begin until the late eighteenth century. His sensibility and storytelling captured people's attention, and by the end of the nineteenth century, his reputation was solidly established. Today, Shakespeare is more widely studied and performed than any other playwright in the Western world, providing a clear testament to the skills and timelessness of the stories told by the Bard.

INTRODUCTION TO THE NOVEL

The following Introduction section is provided solely as an educational tool and is not meant to replace the experience of your reading the work. Read the Introduction and A Brief Synopsis to enhance your understanding of the work and to prepare yourself for the critical thinking that should take place whenever you read any work of fiction or nonfiction. Keep the List of Characters and Character Map at hand so that as you read the original literary work, if you encounter a character about whom you're uncertain, you can refer to the List of Characters and Character Map to refresh your memory.

Introduction

Although it is impossible to date *The Taming of the Shrew* exactly, evidence marks it as one of Shakespeare's earliest comedies, written most likely in the late 1580s or early 1590s. In the Shakespeare chronology, *Shrew* appears to have been written about 8–10 years before *Much Ado About Nothing* (1598), another comedy to which it is often compared. Although the plots themselves are dissimilar, each play gives us a bold and saucy pair of protagonists who enter into a battle of wits. Much of the cleverness and verbal acumen found in *Much Ado* is already apparent in *Shrew*, suggesting that, even early in his career, Shakespeare was extraordinarily skilled in character development, able to pit a headstrong hero and heroine against each other with fantastic results. *Shrew* shows us a dramatist who is sophisticated in his characterization and his ability to deal with multiple plots, as well as to address socially relevant topics, bringing them to the forefront for our consideration and discussion.

The Source for *The Taming of the Shrew*

Like all of Shakespeare's other plays, *The Taming of the Shrew* can be traced to a variety of sources. Unlike most other plays, however, specific texts are difficult to pinpoint. We know that the primary plot, the story of Katherine and Petruchio, finds its roots in folk tales and songs common in Shakespeare's day. In fact, while growing up, Shakespeare was surrounded by a very public debate over the nature of women, including specific arguments on a woman's duty and role in marriage. Shakespeare drew heavily from this debate.

Just as the main story line has its roots in popular debate, so too does the play's Induction. Although inductions were not uncommon in sixteenth- and seventeenth-century dramas, *The Taming of the Shrew* is the only play in which Shakespeare features this particular framing device. For *The Taming of the Shrew*'s Induction, Shakespeare features the tale of a beggar who finds himself mysteriously in power in a rich man's world. Like the tales of shrewish wives, tales of beggars miraculously transformed were featured in a London jest-book (1570) and were commonly featured in sixteenth-century English ballads of which Shakespeare was quite likely familiar.

The Bianca subplot also has its roots in sources with which Shakespeare would have been familiar. Unlike the Kate/Petruchio plot, which can only be traced to general pamphlets and debates, the Bianca subplot comes from George Gascoigne's *Supposes* (1566, 1573), a translation of Ariosto's *I Suppositi* (1509).

Regardless of where Shakespeare drew the basis for the text, the fact remains that he masterfully presents us with a well-founded, carefully developed drama that can't help but get us talking. From the Induction, which seems to end mysteriously and abruptly, to Katherine's final speech on wifely duty, we can't help but find layer upon layer of meaning buried in this early, but great, comedy. Shakespeare uses his skill expertly, bringing out themes we still debate today, over 400 years later.

Shrew's **Performance History**

Largely because of the themes addressed in *The Taming of the Shrew* (marriage, duty, identity, family, and so on), the play has experienced great popularity through the years, although tracing the play's exact performance history is difficult. Little evidence of early productions survives, though we know the play was popular at least into the 1630s. Dramatist John Fletcher created a sequel to Shakespeare's work with his 1611 play *The Woman's Prize, or The Tamer Tamed* wherein Petruchio, now a widower, marries for a second time only to have his wife treat him much the way he initially treated Kate. Aside from contemporary spin-offs, in 1663 the Restoration stage became home to a popular production of Shakespeare's *Shrew*. After 1663, though, *The Taming of the Shrew* slipped off the boards, and we have no record of a production in its original form again until 1844.

In the meantime, however, a number of adaptations flourished. John Lacy's *Sauny the Scot* (1667), a crude farce, was popular for about a century. Although Lacy opted not to include the Christopher Sly scenario, Charles Johnson included it in his 1716 largely political work, *The Cobbler of Preston*. It wasn't until David Garrick's abbreviated version of *Shrew* entitled *Catherine and Petruchio* (1754) that Lacy's *Sauny* was fully replaced. Garrick's work eliminated the Induction, as well as the Bianca subplot. This adaptation also maintained its popularity for about a hundred years. Noted Shakespearean actor John Phillip Kemble also produced an abbreviated version of *Shrew* which competed directly with Garrick's and featured what would become one of Petruchio's trademarks during the eighteenth and nineteenth centuries: cracking a horsewhip to demonstrate his ability as shrew-tamer.

Shakespeare's version of *The Taming of the Shrew* was revived in 1844, over 180 years after it had last been produced. By the end of the nineteenth century, Shakespeare's *Shrew* was favored over adaptations by audiences all over the globe. Since then, *Shrew* has been produced countless times for the stage, as well as for film and television. Although the advent of feminism has caused some audiences to question the relevance of *Shrew*, the play's eternal popularity suggests that this well-written and developed play possesses a timelessness which delights audiences, generation after generation.

Brief Synopsis

The Taming of the Shrew opens with an Induction. Here we meet Christopher Sly, a tinker by trade and a drunk by avocation. As the action opens, he is being thrown out of an alehouse. Drunken, he falls asleep before a nearby Lord's house. When the Lord returns from hunting, he spies Sly and immediately concocts a plan to convince the beggar that he is a nobleman. The Lord orders Sly to be taken into the house, bathed, and placed in the estate's nicest bed. He also orders his servants to wait on Sly and treat him as if *he* were the lord of the manor. In the midst of this merry planning, a troupe of actors appears and is enlisted for a performance that evening.

Upon waking, Christopher Sly is understandably confused. He immediately calls for a drink and is attended to by three servants (supposedly his). The Lord himself assumes a subordinate position and takes great delight at Sly's consternation at the situation. Before long, Sly falls into the Lord's trap and believes he is, in fact, master of all he surveys. The Lord and his servants, though, have a laugh at Sly's expense. When Sly requests his wife join him in bed, he is told that the doctors have warned that sexual activity may cause a relapse, and so rather than risk returning to his beggarly self, he agrees to wait, opting instead to watch the play put on by the acting company.

The story of *The Taming of the Shrew* itself really begins at this point. As Act I opens, we meet Lucentio, a young man who has traveled to Padua from Florence. His servant Tranio accompanies him, and together they secretly witness quite a scene. Before them enters Baptista Minola, his daughters Katherine and Bianca, and two men, Gremio and Hortensio, both wishing to be suitors to Bianca. Minola explains, however, that no one shall court Bianca until her older sister is successfully married. The problem, as the two men point out, is that Kate is so forward and unruly that no one they can think of would possibly want to marry her. Baptista declares he will allow tutors into his house, but no suitors until Kate is wed. After Minola and his entourage leave, Lucentio reveals he has fallen utterly in love with Bianca. Because he knows her father will admit no suitors, he decides to disguise himself as a schoolmaster and secretly court Bianca. Because Lucentio is expected in Padua and his absence would be noted, he instructs his servant Tranio to assume his persona.

Shortly Petruchio, a gentleman from Verona, and his servant Grumio arrive. Petruchio has come seeking his fortune in the form of a wealthy wife. His friend, Hortensio, informs him he knows just the woman, but the drawback is she is a shrew. Petruchio doesn't care. He's sure he can handle the most unruly woman so long as her dowry is ample. Before the two men venture to Minola's house to meet Kate and her father, Hortensio asks Petruchio to presented him to old Baptista as a schoolmaster so he can court Bianca privately. Petruchio agrees and, on their way to Minola's, they meet Gremio who has agreed to present Lucentio (whom he thinks is really Cambio, a tutor who will speak to Bianca on his behalf) to Baptista. Finally, Tranio (disguised as Lucentio), who also wishes to become one of Bianca's suitors, joins the group.

As the second act opens, Kate enters dragging her sister, providing spectators with a peek at what fuels her anger and spite: Bianca is clearly the more favored daughter, and Kate resents it. Soon Baptista enters, and the girls leave. The bevy of suitors arrives, and all men begin to explain their purpose in calling on Minola. He accepts the gifts of tutors and sends them in the house to begin work. He then discusses Kate's dowry with Petruchio and ends by claiming that, when he has won her love, then he may marry her.

Petruchio and Kate's initial meeting features an embittered and passionate volley of insults and slurs, each person meeting the linguistic challenges posited by the other. Petruchio remains undaunted despite Kate's vehement denial of his advances and insists they will be married on Sunday. In order to save face in front of his peers (after all, Kate's putting up a valiant struggle against him), Petruchio explains that Kate is gentle as a lamb in private, but they've agreed she will be shrewd and curst in public. Baptista, satisfied that his eldest daughter has been won, turns his attention to the marriage of his younger daughter, choosing Tranio (Lucentio) as Bianca's groom, provided he can produce proof of the wealth he claims to have. Lucentio and Hortensio, disguised as Cambio and Litio respectively, continue their attempts to woo Bianca as they pretend to instruct her. She clearly prefers Lucentio, although she is cautious in her judgment.

Kate's wedding day approaches, and all the arrangements are made. However, one thing is missing: the groom. When the wedding party waits at the church, wondering if Petruchio will show, Kate is visibly disappointed. When Petruchio finally arrives, he is dressed inappropriately, purposely causing an uproar in his subtle attempt to mirror the senseless bad behavior of his wife-to-be. After the wedding ceremony, Petruchio insists he and Katherine head back to his house immediately, forcing her to miss their own wedding reception. When the newlyweds arrive at Petruchio's house, we hear that they fought the entire way. Upon arriving, Kate is denied food or sleep all under the guise of Petruchio taking especial care of her (no food is good enough nor bed fit enough).

Back at Baptista's house, Hortensio is beginning to realize that Bianca may, in fact, favor his rival, Cambio (the real Lucentio). In his anger, he renounces his pursuit of Bianca and vows to marry a rich widow. He leaves as Tranio enters, informing the lovers of the new development. In order to expedite the marriage of Lucentio and Bianca, though, Tranio needs to find someone to impersonate Vincentio, Lucentio's father, in order to confirm Lucentio's riches. A Pedant approaches and is soon convinced that it would be in his best interest to impersonate Vincentio. Later he will meet with Baptista and convince him that Lucentio (Tranio) is his son and that he does, indeed, possess the riches he claims. When Baptista agrees to the marriage, Biondello informs Cambio (the real Lucentio), and a secret marriage between Bianca and the real Lucentio is arranged.

Back at Petruchio's house, Kate is beginning to lose patience with her husband's seemingly erratic behavior. After his friend Hortensio arrives, Petruchio finally provides Kate with some food but threatens to remove it if she doesn't thank him properly for providing it. Later he proclaims they will return to Padua dressed in the finest array but then rejects the goods of the haberdasher and tailor who were to dress them for their journey. As the party prepares to leave, Petruchio again turns tables on Kate, claiming (purposely in error) that it will be noon when they arrive. When she corrects him (rightly), he calls the trip off until such a time as she obeys what he says. Once they finally get underway, Petruchio still holds fast to his power. He claims the sun is the moon and refuses to let the travelling party continue until Kate agrees with him. She begins to see how Petruchio's system works: If she agrees with him, she gets something she wants. She is tested when Petruchio calls an old man (the real Vincentio) a young woman. Kate agrees, much to Hortensio and Vincentio's befuddlement, and her real transformation begins.

Upon arriving in Padua, Vincentio finds a man masquerading as him, and the disguises begin to become unraveled. After all the impersonators have been found out, the play ends with a banquet in honor of all the newlyweds: Kate and Petruchio, Bianca and Lucentio, and the Widow and Hortensio. As the feast is winding down, the women adjourn, and the men begin to wager on who has the most obedient wife. They wager 100 crowns, each man sure his wife will come when he calls. Lucentio calls for Bianca but she refuses to come. Hortensio calls for the Widow, but she refuses as well. Petruchio calls for Kate, and much to everyone's deep surprise and amazement, she comes directly. She then astounds everyone by not only following Petruchio's instructions to the letter but also offering a long and important speech on a woman's duty to her husband. The play ends with the banquet guests stunned at what they have just witnessed while the newly tamed Kate and Petruchio leave the party together.

List of Characters

Christopher Sly A beggar featured in the Induction. He is tricked into believing he is a gentleman.

A Lord A gentleman who delights in duping Sly after he finds him passed out on his property.

A page, servants, huntsmen All work for or with the Lord to dupe Sly.

Players A travelling troupe of actors who perform the play of Katherine and Petruchio before Sly, the Lord, and the Lord's household.

Katherine Minola Elder daughter of Baptista Minola. She is hard-headed, stubborn, and prone to speaking her mind. Baptista decrees that as the elder daughter, Kate must marry before her younger sister Bianca may do so.

Petruchio A young man of Verona. Through his friend Hortensio, he learns of Katherine and agrees to wed her (for her dowry). What was originally a business venture, though, turns to love as the story unfolds.

Bianca Minola Younger daughter of Baptista Minola. Bianca is loved by Gremio, Hortensio, and Lucentio but cannot have serious suitors or marry until her older sister Katherine has done so. Bianca is clearly Baptista's favorite daughter, although she may not be as sweet as she appears.

Baptista Minola The father of Katherine and Bianca.

Hortensio A suitor to Bianca. He enters the Minola household disguised as Litio, the music tutor. Eventually, he marries the Widow.

Lucentio Son of Vincentio. He is in love with Bianca and woos her disguised as Cambio, the tutor.

Tranio A servant to Lucentio. He agrees to impersonate his master and pretend to woo Bianca for him while Lucentio is disguised as Cambio.

Gremio A foolish old man; suitor to Bianca.

Grumio Petruchio's servant.

Biondello A servant to Lucentio.

Vincentio A gentleman of Pisa; father of Lucentio.

A Pedant A teacher from Mantua. He agrees to impersonate Vincentio for Tranio (unaware he is disguising himself as Lucentio).

A Widow A rich woman whom Hortensio marries after he loses Bianca. She is contemptuous of Kate but also shrewish in her own way.

Character Map

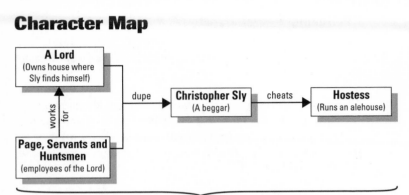

A Lord
(Owns house where Sly finds himself)

works for

Page, Servants and Huntsmen
(employees of the Lord)

dupe → **Christopher Sly** (A beggar)

cheats → **Hostess** (Runs an alehouse)

All watch a play featuring the following players:

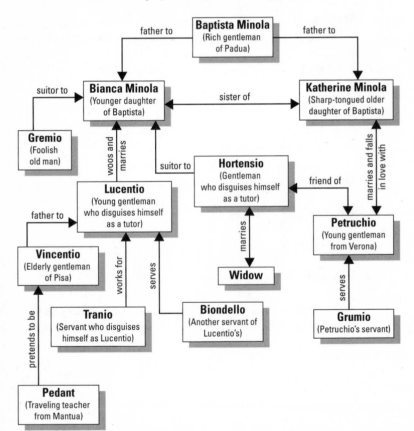

Baptista Minola (Rich gentleman of Padua)

father to

father to

Bianca Minola (Younger daughter of Baptista)

sister of

Katherine Minola (Sharp-tongued older daughter of Baptista)

suitor to

Gremio (Foolish old man)

woos and marries

suitor to

Hortensio (Gentleman who disguises himself as a tutor)

friend of

marries and falls in love with

Lucentio (Young gentleman who disguises himself as a tutor)

father to

Petruchio (Young gentleman from Verona)

marries

Widow

Vincentio (Elderly gentleman of Pisa)

works for

serves

Tranio (Servant who disguises himself as Lucentio)

Biondello (Another servant of Lucentio's)

serves

Grumio (Petruchio's servant)

pretends to be

Pedant (Traveling teacher from Mantua)

CRITICAL COMMENTARIES

The sections that follow provide great tools for supplementing your reading of *The Taming of the Shrew*. First, in order to enhance your understanding of and enjoyment from reading, we provide quick summaries in case you have difficulty when you read the original literary work. Each summary is followed by commentary: literary devices, character analyses, themes, and so on. Keep in mind that the interpretations here are solely those of the author of this study guide and are used to jumpstart your thinking about the work. No single interpretation of a complex work like *The Taming of the Shrew* is infallible or exhaustive, and you'll likely find that you interpret portions of the work differently from the author of this study guide. Read the original work and determine your own interpretations, referring to these Notes for supplemental meanings only.

Induction
Scene 1

Summary

Christopher Sly, a beggar, is tossed out of an alehouse because of his disruptive behavior and quickly falls asleep in front of a Lord's house. When the Lord returns from hunting, he decides to have some fun at Sly's expense and quickly devises a plan to have his household convince Sly that he is a lord, rather than a beggar. Sly is placed in the finest chamber and dressed in the finest clothes so that he will be convinced that he owns the lavish setting in which he finds himself. Should Sly not believe he is and always has been lord of the estate, he is to be told he was ill and had lost his memory. While Sly sleeps off his binge, a group of players appears and are quickly enlisted in the Lord's duping of Sly. He requests they perform a play later that evening (which will mark the play we have come to think of as *The Taming of the Shrew*). The Lord enlists his servant Bartholomew's help in making Sly's duping complete. Bartholomew is to disguise himself as a gentlewoman and pretend to be Sly's wife.

Commentary

An induction is traditionally "an introduction; preface or prelude," a definition which easily fits what Shakespeare is doing here. However, an induction can also be "a bringing forward of separate facts or instances, [especially] so as to prove a general statement." In many ways, this, too, is what Shakespeare is doing. *The Taming of the Shrew*'s Induction leads us into the play proper, as the first definition suggests, but it does much more than that. In keeping with the latter definition, the Induction cleverly introduces several key themes such as identity, disguise, illusion, and reality which are developed fully in the play itself. Because we are introduced to these themes from the very beginning, we are consciously and unconsciously preparing ourselves to look for them as the action unfolds.

Theme

Although the Induction may seem merely a precursor to the play itself, it is more cleverly conceived than that. It invites audiences to consider individual identities and whether or not people can either impersonate others (generally of another class—inferior to superior or vice versa) or, in the case of Christopher Sly, be convinced that he is someone other than who he is. It is as if Shakespeare is winking to us from the play's onset, telling us we'd better be on the lookout because we'll soon find things are not quite what they seem! If we miss his early warning, we'll find ourselves duped, and the joke will be on us.

Because the story set forth in the Induction is not carried throughout the entirety of *The Taming of the Shrew*, it is often cut or minimized in performance. Such a decision, though, undermines some of the key messages of the play, especially those related to notions of identity and disguise. However, the lack of follow-through with the Induction is admittedly a fault of the play—at least in the version we have inherited. Scholars theorize that another version of this play no longer extant ended with a return to Christopher Sly, bringing the Induction full circle.

Sly, himself, is an interesting character. We see little of him in the first scene of the Induction because he passes out by the fourteenth line and is not heard from until the Induction's second scene. However, the brief glimpse we get quickly establishes him as a drunken, belligerent sot unwilling to settle up with the Hostess. His initial lines show he is a comic, buffoon-like character (such as we would later see in *Much Ado About Nothing*'s Constable Dogberry), unable to string an accurate sentence together and destined to become the butt of jokes. Sly tells the Hostess "The Slys are no rogues . . . we came in with Richard Conqueror" (3–4). Of course, Sly really means William the Conqueror. Next, he quibbles on the Hostess's declaration she will fetch the constable. Although his next action is to fall asleep, we can be sure Sly will provide great entertainment down the road.

The Lord's entrance sets the plan to dupe Sly into motion and introduces the notion of illusion to the story. The Lord, as if having nothing better to do, creates a comic inversion, enlisting the assistance of the entire household. His desire to take the drunken Sly and give him every luxury of a lord in an attempt to make "the beggar then forget himself" (40) goes far to address a very real concern for Elizabethan audiences. In Shakespeare's day, great discussion surrounded the idea of what we would now term "social mobility." In short, those in power wanted to keep the power and part of how they did that was by attempting to prevent others from dressing (and therefore acting) out-side their birth. The underlying fear was that one born into a lower class could, by assuming proper clothes, pass oneself off as a social superior. Of course, as the Lord and Sly show us in Scene 2 of the Induction, the clothes alone do not make the man—at least not when an inferior attempts to take the place of a superior.

Of particular interest is the Lord's ordering his man Bartholomew to take on the role of Sly's wife, doting over him and even crying when appropriate (with help of an onion, if needed). Of course, the joke would have been entirely clear to Shakespeare's audience, who would have been all too aware that *all* women on the British public stage were played by boys and young men. In addition to calling direct attention to one of the most hotly debated aspects of the stage, Shakespeare also uses Bartholomew to introduce us to the idea of marital accord (or discord, as the case may be). The next scene of the Induction features Bartholomew and Sly interacting, giving us the first of what will eventually be many views on the subject of marriage. This time, however, we can't miss the comic effect. Shakespeare has made sure we are in on the joke.

Glossary

(Here and in the following glossary sections, difficult words and phrases, as well as allusions and historical references, are explained.)

paucas pallabris (5)   In Modern Spanish, pocas palabras means "few words."

denier (8)   a small, obsolete French coin of little value.

third-borough (10)   constable.

"Breathe Merriman—the poor cur is embossed" (16)   "Let the dog, Merriman, breathe. The poor dog is foaming at the mouth from exhaustion."

diaper (56)   a napkin or towel.

"husbanded with modesty" (67)   "managed with decorum."

overeying (94)   witnessing.

veriest antic (100)   oddest buffoon or eccentric.

buttery (101)   a place where the food supplies of a household are kept; pantry.

Induction
Scene 2

Summary

Christopher Sly awakes to find himself in a lovely bedchamber in a strange house (the Lord's) with attendants ready to wait on him. Bewildered, Sly calls for a drink. As Sly attempts to figure out what has happened, the serving men reassure him that the entire household is overjoyed to learn their master has made a miraculous recovery after having been ill the past fifteen years. In getting Sly ready to meet the others in the house, the serving men regale him with fanciful stories of all the harsh dreams of poverty brought about by his madness. Sly is drawn into the tale the servants weave, and, by the time his supposed "wife" enters, he is completely convinced he is, in fact, lord of the estate. He beckons his wife to come to bed with him, but Bartholomew handily escapes by noting the doctor has not recommended such activity in case of a relapse. To pass the time, however, the players agree to entertain the group with a story. Sly, Bartholomew, and the others settle in for the performance.

Commentary

When Sly awakes, the Lord's plan goes into full swing. The servingmen dote on the beggar, insisting he is, in fact, lord of all he surveys. Sly's immediate response is, of course, disbelief. Our first glimpse of Sly revealed a man who uttered four lines and passed out. Not surprisingly, his first action in this scene is to call for "a pot of small ale" (1). In addition to revealing his predilection for liquor, Sly's request reveals his social status. Accustomed to having very little money, he calls for a cheap drink. When the serving men encourage "[his] lordship" to drink "sack" and taste of the "conserves" (2–3), we begin to see just how much out of his element Sly is—and he knows it.

With an obvious lack of decorum Sly informs the serving men he is neither "[his] honor" nor "lordship" (5–6). He continues, disparaging sack and conserves, two of the pleasures of the upper class, and then very wittily confesses there is no need to ask what he wants to wear because he has only one set of clothes, so there is little choice to be made. Clearly at this point, Sly is in control of his identity. He knows who he is and remembers his accustomed lifestyle. In fact, in many ways, Sly deserves respect because he is initially skeptical about the situation in which he finds himself. However, it doesn't take long before the rhetoric of the Lord and his servants begins to take ahold of Sly (but who could blame him? In many ways, for a poor man to wake up rich is a dream come true).

When the Lord enters (13), the duping really picks up steam. Blaming Sly's seemingly mad behavior on a foul spirit (14–16), the Lord begins to talk Sly into believing he really is of the gentry rather than, as Sly himself confesses, "by birth a peddler, by education a cardmaker, by transmutation a bearherd, and now by present profession a tinker" (18–20). Sly humorously exposes his true self in an attempt to clarify the situation by suggesting the Lord call upon Marian Hacket who definitely will confirm he's in debt.

In response to Sly's objections, the Lord and his men continue to sway Sly with their rhetoric. Lunacy, they allege, is the reason Sly mistakenly believes he is a beggar. The whole house, they claim, rejoices in his recovery but is saddened by the mad illusion Sly has awakened with. The servingmen continue to ply Sly with suggestions for entertainments and luxuries he might enjoy. When they suggest to Sly he has a wife "more beautiful/ Than any woman in this waning age" (62–63), he begins to show signs of believing them. Sly's confusion is revealed in his remark "Am I a lord? And have I such a lady? / Or do I dream? Or have I dreamed till now?" (68–69). Just as the Lord intends, Sly is being taken in by the illusion in which he finds himself.

Despite Sly's growing suspicion that he may, in fact, be a lord after all, we are in on the joke and see over and over how, although Sly may dress the part, there is no real risk of him being able successfully to pass himself off as gentry. In addition to the incredulous story of fifteen years' illness (which the gullible Sly swallows hook, line, and sinker), Sly's language and behavior suggest that there is more to being a gentleman than having fine clothes and being able to order servants around. When Bartholomew the page enters, feigning concern for Sly as his wife, Sly first wonders why his wife calls him "noble lord" rather than "husband" since he is her "goodman"(101–102). His terminology sets up interesting and telling distinctions.

In the class from which Sly originally comes, "Lord" is a term used by men for men. "Lord" is also a term a woman of the upper class would apply to her spouse more readily than a woman of the lower class, who would likely call her husband "goodman." Next, Sly questions what to call his wife. What he's seeking is, quite simply, her name. Because he was raised in a lesser social class, Sly must be informed by the real Lord that his "wife" is to be addressed as "Madam, and nothing else. So lords call ladies" (108).

Sly then continues to show his natural biases and base nature by demanding his "wife" undress and come to bed (112). While on one hand this demand is outrageously funny (because we know the page is really playing Sly's supposed wife), it is also quite revealing. We get a good sense of what Sly's about—and more importantly, how he perceives marriage roles, something that will be picked up in more detail in the play. Sly's initial instinct to control and command his wife, however, yields him nothing. Bartholomew is quick to say "your physicians have expressly charged, / In peril to incur your former malady, / That I should yet absent me from your bed" (118–120). Sly, clearly believing himself to be the lord of the manor, doesn't wish to risk a relapse, and so he releases his wife from her "duties."

At this point the players enter again, bringing us toward the beginning of the actual play. With only one small reference at the end of Act I, Scene 1, the story of Sly is left behind, leaving us to wonder what became of him.

Glossary

small ale (1)   weak (and therefore cheap) ale.

sack (2)   any of various dry white wines from Spain or the Canary Islands, popular in England during the sixteenth and seventeenth centuries.

conserves (3)   a kind of jam made of two or more fruits, often with nuts or raisins added.

cardmaker (19)   maker of cards, or combs, used to prepare wool for spinning.

"on the score" (23)   "in debt."

bestraught (24)   distracted.

Semiramis (39)   a queen of Assyria noted for her beauty, wisdom, and sexual exploits: reputed founder of Babylon: based on a historical queen of the ninth century B.C.

welkin (45)   the vault of heaven, the sky, or the upper air.

course (47)   hunt the hare.

Adonis (50)   in Greek myth, a handsome young man loved by Aphrodite: he is killed by a wild boar.

Cytherea (51)   Aphrodite.

sedges (51)   any of the plants of the sedge family often found on wet ground or in water, having usually triangular, solid stems, three rows of narrow, pointed leaves, and minute flowers borne in spikelets.

Io (54)   a maiden loved by Zeus and changed into a heifer by jealous Hera or, in some tales, by Zeus to protect her: she is watched by Argus and is driven to Egypt, where she regains human form.

Daphne (57)   a nymph who is changed into a laurel tree to escape Apollo's advances.

Apollo (59)   the god of music, poetry, prophecy, and medicine, represented as exemplifying manly youth and beauty: later identified with Helios.

"present her at the leet" (87)   "bring accusation against [the Hostess] at the manorial court."

Amends (97)   recovery.

Act I
Scene 1

Summary

Shakespeare's play proper opens with Lucentio, a Florentine traveler who has come to study in Padua, and his servant Tranio. Upon their arrival, they see Baptista Minola, a rich gentleman of Padua, approaching with his two daughters, Katherine and her younger sister Bianca, as well as Gremio and Hortensio, both suitors to Bianca. Baptista is in the process of rejecting both suitors for Bianca because Katherine must wed before he will allow her younger sister to do so. Kate is a sharp-tongued young woman, and, based on the remarks of Hortensio and Gremio, it does not seem likely she will easily acquire a husband, thereby lessening their chances of ever being with Bianca. Both men agree to do their best to find Katherine a husband so that they may have a chance at winning the younger, more beautiful and desirable daughter, Bianca.

Lucentio himself has fallen hopelessly in love with Bianca. Lucentio devises a plan to bring him closer to Bianca while appearing to honor her father's wishes: He proposes to disguise himself as a schoolmaster and thereby work his way into the Minola household. Tranio reminds his master that he is expected in Padua and, if he doesn't arrive, trouble will arise. As a remedy to this potential problem, Lucentio quickly dictates Tranio impersonate him while he is disguised as a tutor—a ruse that is sure to work since no one in Padua has ever met either of them. Another of Lucentio's servants, Biondello, arrives and is confused at seeing Tranio dressed in his master's clothes. Lucentio tells Biondello Tranio has agreed to impersonate him because he has killed a man in Padua and his life is on the line.

Commentary

As Act I opens, Shakespeare wastes no time in addressing themes that he has used to entice us in the Induction. Disguise, deception, love, marriage, and power all come to the forefront in this short but forceful scene. Baptista finds himself surrounded by an assortment of suitors for his younger daughter, Bianca, and forms the crux of the play's action by insisting on the time-honored tradition of the eldest child marrying first. Bianca quickly comes off as desirable, perfectly embodying everything men (and the society they dominate) deem as profitable in a woman: modesty, beauty, passivity. The obstacle standing in the way of the would-be suitors gaining the woman who would, quite literally, be their prize is her older and more boisterous sister: Katherine.

When we meet Kate, she seems fairly innocuous. Upon hearing her father's decree that she marry before Bianca, Kate offers a witty reply, questioning whether her father will "make a stale of [her] amongst these mates?" (58). Her reply is telling in two regards. First, it shows her facility with language, a customarily male trait, setting her up outside the womanly norm. We know from her clever punning on the notion of a stalemate that she is not going to be a stereotypically "good" woman (meaning: passive and controlled). Second, her remark reveals a bit about her judgment. Although we know from what Gremio and Hortensio say that Kate is perceived as devilish, headstrong, and wild, Kate's remarks reveal that she may not be as bad as they suggest. Her outright contempt for Bianca's would-be suitors is bold, to be sure, but not entirely unwarranted. In fact, in one light, it speaks well of her judgment.

Although the male characters, especially Gremio and Hortensio, call Kate disparaging names such as "fiend of hell" (88), Shakespeare allows for the possibility that Kate is not as terrible as they would have us believe—rather, she is independent and headstrong, but with some justifiable cause. Neither would make a good match for Kate: Gremio himself is termed "a pantaloon" (s.d. 48), a foolish old man who is a stock character type in *commedia dell'arte* dramas. Hortensio, too, does not come off as a prize catch, although he *is* somewhat better than Gremio; Hortensio's personality, though, is weak and effeminate.

In stark contrast to Kate stands her sister, Bianca. Her name alone evokes whiteness, purity, and other such ethereal connotations. The opening scene does much to stress Bianca's angelic whiteness, her purity, and her virginal nature. She is clearly Baptista's favored daughter and is able to inspire instant love and longing from the men who see her. She draws suitors young and old, and, were it not for her sister (whom society deems undesirable because of her lack of demurity), she would have her pick of suitors. A woman who so readily inspires admiration through her beauty and her passivity, though, bears watching as the play unfolds.

Act I, Scene 1 also introduces us to Baptista, the family patriarch. As the leader of the Minola family, he is in a precarious position. On one hand, he has a lovely daughter who inspires the admiration of men. With the right marriage, he could easily increase the family fortune and status. There is one impediment, however—Katherine. As patriarch, Baptista knows the elder daughter is to marry first. As patriarch, he also has the option of disregarding convention. The risk? Potential public disgrace and ruin. However, the prospects for Kate do not look good, increasing the complexity of Baptista's position. While he waits for Kate to meet and marry her match, Baptista has the (seemingly) good sense to provide for his daughters. His willingness to have them tutored in music, poetry, and other academic subjects speaks well of his role as a father.

Lucentio, overhearing the whole exchange between Baptista, his daughters, and Bianca's would-be suitors, has fallen immediately in love with Bianca. Of course to us this seems entirely incredulous, but love at first sight is a common element to romantic farces such as *The Taming of the Shrew*. Lucentio, in fact, takes on elements of a stock character type himself: the courtly lover. In words reminiscent of Chaucer's "Knight's Tale" or the story of Pyramus and Thisbe, Lucentio recounts how the sudden sight of Bianca "hath thralled [his] wounded eye" (221). In keeping with the tradition of courtly love, Lucentio's wound is not initially in his heart, but in his eye, that organ through which he first espied his love. Lucentio borders on becoming a parody of courtly love as he provides a fairly full cataloguing of Bianca's beauty and its effect on him. He praises her modesty, as well as the "sweet beauty in her face" (168), "her coral lips" (175), her breath which did "perfume the air" (176), and her all around "sacred and sweet" nature (177). To his credit, he also feels the proper Petrarchan responses to Bianca's beauty. He laments that he burns, pines, and perishes (156), consumed by his aching love for Baptista's younger daughter. Lucentio becomes, in effect, the quintessential courtly lover and will later be starkly contrasted with not only Petruchio's motivation for marriage but also the primitive and powerful taming techniques Petruchio later uses.

Finally, the important theme of disguise is also advanced in this scene. By the end of the scene, we have a total of four people assuming disguise (Sly and Bartholomew in the Induction; Lucentio and Tranio in Act I, Scene 1). The disguises so far have been overt and sartorial in nature; people assume physical disguises in attempt to pass themselves off as someone else. Seeing so many people assuming identities reminds us that *The Taming of the Shrew* is a comedy of mistaken and disguised identity—a theme that will become increasingly more complex (yet increasingly subtle) as the play unfolds.

Glossary

"Mi perdonate" (25)   "Pardon me."

Aristotle's checks (32)   constraining philosophic study of Aristotle.

balk logic (34)   argue.

affect (40)   find pleasant.

iwis (62)   certainly; assuredly.

"comb your noddle" (64)   "rake your head."

Minerva (84)   the [Roman] goddess of wisdom, technical skill, and invention: identified with the Greek Athena.

mew (87)   confine in or as in a cage; shut up or conceal: often with up.

"had as lief" (132)   "would as willingly."

"bar in law" (136)   "legal impediment."

Anna (155)   confidante of her sister Dido, Queen of Carthage, beloved of Aeneas.

"Redime te captum quam queas minimo" (163)   "Buy yourself out of bondage for as little as you can."

Daughter of Agenor (169)   Europa, beloved of Jove.

"Basta!" (199)   "Enough!"

port (204)   the manner in which one carries oneself; carriage.

"uncase thee" (208)   get undressed.

Act I
Scene 2

Summary

Petruchio and his servant, Grumio, enter. Petruchio has come from Verona to Padua to seek his fortune. He arrives at his old friend Hortensio's house and fills Hortensio in on his financial situation. Hortensio jokingly asks Petruchio whether he would like a shrewish, yet rich, wife. Petruchio assures his friend that no woman could be too shrewish, too unattractive, or too hard to handle, as long as her dowry was sufficient and swears that day to make Katherine his. As Petruchio prepares to head to Minola's, Hortensio volunteers to accompany him because "in Baptista's keep [his] treasure is" (117). Since Bianca's father refuses to let her have suitors, Hortensio asks Petruchio to offer him, "disguised in sober robes" (131), as a music instructor to Bianca so that he might court her secretly.

Gremio arrives with Lucentio (disguised as a schoolmaster). In offering Lucentio as a tutor to Baptista's daughters, Gremio's real plan is to have the scholar (Lucentio) sing his praises to Bianca. When all the men meet, Hortensio informs Gremio that he, too, has found a tutor to send to the Minola's. He also informs Gremio he has also found a man who "will undertake to woo curst Katherine, / Yea, and to marry her, if her dowry please" (182–183). Petruchio, undaunted by the horrific tales of Kate, assures the men she will be easily won. As the scene ends, Tranio (disguised as Lucentio) appears with Biondello as they, too, head to Minola's house. Tranio informs Gremio and Hortensio that he, too, shall be considered as a suitor for Bianca.

Commentary

Shakespeare, after carefully setting up his story through the Induction and the opening scene, finally allows us to have more than a momentary look at one of the story's protagonists—however, it isn't Katherine Minola we see. Instead, Shakespeare shifts his focus away from the woman who will be at the heart of the comedy and directs our attention to Petruchio, a Veronese man who has come to Padua on a mission: to "wive it wealthily in Padua; / If wealthily, then happily in Padua" (74–75). Unlike Katherine, whom we learn about largely through the questionably biased perspectives of other characters (she speaks only thirteen lines in all of Act I—hardly enough for us to determine whether she really is a shrew or not), Petruchio appears and through his own account, we learn more about his motivation.

The initial encounter with Petruchio reveals a young man of some means who is traveling through Padua with his servant, as if on a quest. Indeed, he does seek an elusive prize—fortune. His witty banter reveals a quick mind and an even quicker tongue (although his servant Grumio does a fine job of keeping up with his master), both traits he'll need if he is to go against Baptista's shrewish daughter. Petruchio is not a tolerant man, though he is by no means an ogre. His quibble with Grumio rapidly escalates to physical confrontation, demonstrating he is not a man afraid to use force to get his point across. Petruchio is used to holding a dominant position, and his treatment of Gremio serves as a warning of that which he is capable.

Upon meeting Hortensio, an old friend, Petruchio recounts his situation and what brings him to Padua. His status, we find, is not terribly unlike other sons. After his father's death, he has come into his inheritance. "Crowns in my purse I have, and goods at home," Petruchio declares (56), but we must not read too much into that confession. Just prior he has noted his overarching goal is "Happily to wive and thrive as best I may" (55). Some critics theorize that although Petruchio has come into his inheritance, it is not of considerable quantity, and therefore he needs the financial resources of a wealthy wife in order to secure his position as one of the up and coming gentry. Hortensio seems to be aware of his friend's precarious status because he immediately, albeit half-comically, offers to fix him up with someone who is assuredly rich, although she is also hard to handle and most likely not worth even the largest fortune. Petruchio's ears immediately perk up at Hortensio's offer, and he shows us just how ready he is to marry for money.

Although Petruchio's motives may seem a bit mercenary to us today when we espouse marrying for love, at the time in which the play was written, marriage for reasons other than love was not at all unusual. Political alliances and family fortunes were often at the heart of marriages, especially in the upper classes from which people like Petruchio and Kate come. Petruchio is clearly interested in solidifying his net worth, and how better to do it than through marriage? Kate, the elder daughter of a wealthy man who has no sons (nor any promise of ever having any) is a prime catch. She brings a generous dowry and stands to inherit half her father's worth upon his death. Her personality has kept suitors from capitalizing on her economic potential, but we must wonder, given what mercenary tactics may underlay marriage, perhaps Kate's behavior is merely a defense against men seeking her fortune rather than her company (an issue which is explored further in Act II).

Shakespeare has set up two distinctly volatile personalities in Petruchio and Katherine. Although what we know of Kate so far comes largely through what other's say of her, we know her well enough to know that if their accounts are even partially correct, the action will explode when she meets Petruchio.

Just as the theme of marriage, its purposes and forms, expands in this scene, so too does the number of disguises. Hortensio, rejected as a suitor to Bianca, is determined to work his way into Baptista Minola's house. In disguising himself as a music tutor, he believes, as does Lucentio, that he can get the upper hand on the competition for Bianca's love. What he doesn't realize, of course, is that Lucentio has the same plan. (In reality, Hortensio doesn't even know Lucentio is his competition. Hortensio believes Gremio is his only rival.) Shakespeare makes sure to let the audience in on the joke, allowing us to wait for comic moment when the two tutors are welcomed into Baptista's house.

Character Insight

In Act I, Scene 2, we again meet Gremio, accompanied this time by Lucentio. At his second appearance in so many scenes, spectators again see Gremio's comic flatness. His lack of depth serves two distinct purposes. First it makes it impossible to identify with him and, in turn, makes Lucentio's plan to best him quite comic. Rather than doing Gremio's bidding as he is supposed to do when, disguised as a tutor, he enters the Minola household, we know Lucentio will be advancing his own case as Bianca's suitor. We have little sympathy for Gremio. Instead, we smile to see such a ridiculous old man exercising such poor judgment in his quest for a beautiful young girl. The comic flatness of Gremio also keeps spectators firmly aware that what is unfolding on the stage is, in fact, a comedy, not a slice of life (information that will need to be remembered in Act V).

Glossary

trow (4)   to believe, think, suppose, etc.

"Con tutto il cuore ben trovato" (24)   "With all my heart, well met."

"Alla nostra casa ben venuto, / Molto oronato signor mio Petruchio" (25–26)   "Welcome to our house, my much honored Petruchio."

compound (27)   to settle by mutual agreement.

pip (33)   any of the suit-indicating figures on playing cards, or any of the dots on dice or dominoes.

"come roundly" (58)   "speak plainly."

burden (67)   a repeated, central idea; theme.

Florentius (68)   a knight in John Gower's *Confessio Amantis* who promises to marry an ugly old woman if she solves the riddle he must answer. After fulfilling the promise, she becomes young and beautiful.

Sibyl (69)   prophetess to whom Apollo gave as many years of life as she held grains of sand in her hand.

Xanthippe (70)   fifth century B.C.; wife of Socrates: the prototype of the quarrelsome, nagging wife.

grace (130)   goodwill; favor.

"mend it with a largess" (149)   "improve with a gift or gifts given in a generous, or sometimes showy, way."

ordnance (202)   cannon or artillery.

'larums (205)   alarums; calls to arms.

Leda's daughter (242)   Helen of Troy.

Paris (245)   a son of Priam, king of Troy: his kidnapping of Helen, wife of Menelaus, causes the Trojan War.

jade (247)   a horse, especially a worn-out, worthless one.

Alcides' twelve (256)   reference to the twelve labors of Hercules (reputed grandson of Alcaeus).

quaff carouses (275)   drink toasts.

Act II
Scene 1

Summary

The action shifts back to Baptista Minola and his daughters. Katherine enters, dragging her sister behind her, and proceeds to question Bianca about which man she loves. Bianca, a bit frightened by her sister's actions, offers to give Kate whichever man she wants. Their father enters and tries to placate the fighting sisters. He chastises Kate cruelly and rescues Bianca, wondering why he is plagued by such an unruly daughter.

Gremio, Lucentio (disguised), Petruchio, Hortensio (disguised), Tranio (disguised), and Biondello enter. Petruchio announces his intent to court Kate and presents Hortensio (disguised as Litio) as a music tutor to the two women. Seeing Baptista's easy acceptance of Litio's services, Gremio quickly advances his man, Cambio (the disguised Lucentio), as a scholar for Baptista's daughters. He, too, is welcomed into the house. Tranio announces himself as a suitor for Bianca; then the two tutors are taken inside to begin their work.

Petruchio claims he is ready to draw up the marriage contract, but Baptista insists he must first get Kate's love. As Petruchio and Baptista discuss the likelihood of Petruchio's wooing successfully, Hortensio re-enters with his lute hanging around his head, courtesy of Kate. When Petruchio and Kate are finally left alone, Petruchio insists Kate is the most demure, lovely woman on earth, but she is not drawn in by his rhetoric. They banter and exchange quips until Kate, having had enough, hits Petruchio. He does not strike her back but threatens he will do so, if need be. Petruchio remains undaunted in his quest for a wealthy wife, though, and vows to marry her despite her obvious objections.

When the men return to check on Petruchio's progress, he announces the wedding will be on Sunday. Kate raises her voice in protest, which leads Petruchio to make up a story about how in private Kate is coy and gentle but they have come to an agreement that "she shall be curst in company" (303). Baptista agrees to the match and Petruchio exits.

Baptista then turns his attention to Bianca's suitors. Gremio and Tranio vie for her by outlining for Baptista all they can offer her. Whatever Gremio offers, Tranio offers more, until Baptista has no choice but to accept Tranio's dower, provided he can provide proof that he does, in fact, possess the riches he claims. Tranio now realizes that he must get someone to impersonate Vincentio, Lucentio's father, in order to continue the masquerade and win Bianca for his master.

Commentary

Act II, Scene 1 is the longest scene in all of *The Taming of the Shrew*. In fact, it comprises the entire act. It is, as its size alone would dictate, an important scene and does much to advance both the story's action and the characterizations of the principle players. In it both daughters are betrothed (although not yet wed), and the primary disguises are set in place.

Character Insight

The first person we learn more of is Kate. In fact, this is our first real opportunity to see her for ourselves, and, once we are able to judge for ourselves, we see that, although she may behave rudely, even viciously at places, there is an obvious reason for her behavior. Her confrontation with Bianca in the scene's opening lines makes clear two important elements of her character. First, we see that Kate does, quite likely, want to be wed. Her attack on Bianca is essentially precipitated because Bianca has an abundance of suitors while Kate has none. Compounded on top of this is Baptista's clear preference for Bianca. He calls Kate a "hilding of a devilish spirit" (26) and wonders what he has ever done to be "thus grieved as I" (37). Is it any wonder Kate rebels against her father? Together they seem to be caught in an endless cycle of dysfunction; the more he favors Bianca, the more Kate acts defiantly, causing him to favor Bianca. Kate even goes so far as to call her father on his favoritism (31–36) and seethingly waits until she can "find occasion of revenge" (36).

Kate and Petruchio's private exchange also gives us a clearer indication of what each of these characters is like. Katherine, to be sure, has never met up with a man like Petruchio before. She insults him, and he speaks sweetly. She goads him, and he offers clever replies. She belittles him, and still she is treated with patience and kind words (granted, they are occasionally delivered a bit sarcastically). Kate is used to throwing a tantrum and either being punished and spoken harshly to, or getting her own way. How unusual that someone would treat her differently.

It is only when she strikes Petruchio that she is able to vary his response. He does not strike out at her but warns if she hits him again he will strike back. Apparently the warning is enough, for she does not resort to physical violence again in this scene.

Just as Kate gains more depth, Petruchio's character is also developed more in this scene. Petruchio, anxious to secure his wealthy wife, is willing to draw up the marriage contracts—or "specialties" (126)—before having even seen Katherine. He is obviously confident in his ability to withstand Kate's purported wrath. What we see, though, when the two *do* actually come into contact with each other, is that, despite his original intention to marry purely for the money, there is an underlying attraction between the two. Before he even meets her, in fact, he's beginning to like her unconventional ways. When Hortensio enters, broken lute about his head, Petruchio remarks "it is a lusty wench! / I love her ten time more than e'er I did. / O, how I long to have some chat with her!" (160–162). Of course, the claim could be made that he's trying too hard to make a good impression on the men (showing he's not at all afraid of what he's getting into), but it seems more likely that he is inwardly pleased to see Kate is a woman of high spirits.

Later in the scene, after being rejoined by Baptista, Gremio, and Tranio, Petruchio again shows us he is a quick and clever thinker. His highly comic lie about how, in private Kate "hung about [his] neck" (306) but in public she's agreed she'll be "curst" (303) brings the story's key theme of public behavior and private behavior to the forefront. Although in reality, he's merely concocting a story of what has just happened, placing himself in a good light, there's more truth in what he says than we may realize. The distinction between what denotes proper *public* behavior and how that may or may not differ from *private* behavior will drive the play, especially Act V. Petruchio's lie, too, makes it readily apparent he's the only man in the story so far who has the *wit* to compete with Kate.

Just as Petruchio and Kate become more dimensional in this scene, so too, does Baptista gain more depth. We know he's a good provider for his family, although not, perhaps, the most fair of fathers. He seems quite realistic about the difficulties Petruchio will have courting Kate but is willing to let him try. To Baptista's credit, though, he seems to be willing to reject Kate's only suitor if that suitor cannot earn her love (128–129). Although this speaks well for Baptista, later in the scene, we see that his concern was not really with his daughter; he agrees to the wedding despite Kate's vocal protestations. With Bianca, too, he sets aside any notion of love, entrusting his favorite daughter to the man who can offer the best dower. Baptista may like to *think* he is above regarding marriage as a commercial enterprise, but his actions suggest a different view. The claim could be advanced that Baptista is merely looking for the best provider for his daughter, but the fact remains that he, too, will benefit, politically and especially economically, by the allegiance his daughter makes.

Gremio and Tranio's bidding war is, in fact, Shakespeare's way of poking fun at an age-old system that is really very much like an auction where the desired object, in this case Bianca, goes to the highest bidder. Part of what makes the bidding so laughable is, of course, that Tranio, a servant, is offering up riches he does not possess. Of course, before the marriage transaction can take place, Baptista will want verification of the riches Tranio offers. But in the meantime, we must smile at the wily servant who continually ups the ante in the bidding war. Eventually, Gremio's riches are exhausted, and so Bianca is promised to Tranio, "if [he] make [his] assurance" (394) or provide proof of what he offers. If not, Gremio shall have Bianca a week after Katherine is wed. Once again we see Baptista is not much different than a merchant wishing to conduct a business transaction. He is eager to marry Bianca to one of her suitors, and, if the man who appears richest turns out not to be so, well then, the next richest will do.

Glossary

affect (14)   love.

belike (16)   perhaps.

hilding (17)   a low, contemptible person.

"suffer me" (31)   "let me have my way."

orderly (45)   in regular or proper order; methodically.

"Bacare!" (73)   "stand back!"

grateful (76)   pleasing.

orchard (111)   garden.

"in possession" (122)   "in immediate possession."

specialties (126)   a special contract, obligation, agreement, etc.

"happy be thy speed" (138)   "may it turn out well for you."

to the proof (140)   in armor.

lusty (160)   full of vigor; strong, robust, hearty, etc.

clear (172)   serene and calm.

banns (180)   the proclamation, generally made in church on three successive Sundays, of an intended marriage.

movable (197)   one easily changed or dissuaded; also a piece of furniture.

joint-stool (198)   a well-fitted stool made by an expert craftsman.

arms (223)   coat of arms.

craven (227)   a thorough coward.

crab (229)   crab apple.

passing (239)   surpassing; extreme; very.

"whom thou keep'st command" (254)   "whom you employ"; that is, servants.

Dian (255)   Diana, the virgin goddess of the moon and of hunting: identified with the Greek Artemis.

Grissel (292)   Griselda; the heroine of various medieval tales, famous for her meek, long-suffering patience.

Lucrece (293)   Lucrecia; Roman lady who took her own life after her chastity had been violated.

vied (307)   bet; wagered.

meacock (311)   cowardly.

"desperate mart" (325)   "risky venture."

jointure (368)   an arrangement by which a husband grants real property to his wife for her use after his death; also, the property thus settled, widow's portion.

argosy (372)   a large ship, especially a merchant ship.

outvied (383)   outbid.

cavil (388)   to object when there is little reason to do so; resort to trivial fault-finding; carp; quibble.

Act III
Scene 1

Summary

Now that Katherine is to be married, our attention shifts to Bianca. Lucentio, disguised as the school teacher Cambio, and Hortensio, disguised as the musician Litio, both vie for Bianca's attention. Knowing nothing of the other man's love for Bianca, each suitor tries to get Bianca for his own. Lucentio and Hortensio quarrel over who should spend time alone with Bianca first. Bianca herself steps in and resolves the dispute, telling Hortensio that while he tunes his instrument, she shall study with Lucentio.

While pretending to study a Latin text, Lucentio confesses his love for Bianca. She gently rebukes him. When Hortensio gets his chance to be alone with Bianca, she is far less receptive to his advances than she was to Lucentio's. When Bianca is called away to help prepare for Kate's wedding, Lucentio accompanies her. Hortensio begins to realize Cambio is in love with Bianca. He vows that if, in fact, Bianca redirects her love to Cambio, he will get even with her by withdrawing his affection of her and placing it on another woman.

Commentary

Shakespeare moves his audience from the frantic and furious wooing style of Petruchio and Kate to the more traditional (yet still somewhat unconventional) wooing practiced by Lucentio and Hortensio. Just as the two sisters contrast in personalities, so too do these two wooing scenes contrast each other.

As Lucentio (as Cambio) and Hortensio (as Litio) vie for Bianca's attention, they continually demonstrate their shallowness and petty jealousies. Because they cannot come to a compromise over who shall be alone with Bianca first, Bianca must step in and resolve the situation. When they do get time alone with her, each attempts to advance his case, only to find it is Bianca who really holds the reigns. In keeping with the notion of courtly love, the woman must reject her suitors' advances. Bianca does so, but for Lucentio, her rebuke is merely protocol, whereas her rebuke of Hortensio is more earnest in nature.

Character Insight

Whereas Lucentio and Hortensio come off as comic lovers in this scene, Bianca shows more signs of strength than we have seen up to this point. She resolves the dispute over whom she will work with first and, as she is having her lessons, appears to be entirely cognizant of the situation unfolding before her. Lucentio's advances, interspersed between Latin phrases, do not escape her attention. Although she clearly prefers Lucentio to Hortensio, she carefully instructs him to "presume not," but softens her admonition with the instruction "despair not" (44). When Hortensio makes his advances under the pretense of teaching her the "gamut," she quickly rebukes him. From this simple act, we see that she is decidedly capable of passing judgment and satisfying her own whims and desires—two traits which, although they give her personality dimension and make her more life-like, would not have been seen as favorable in women of the time.

At scene's end, Hortensio is beginning to realize he may not become Bianca's chosen suitor and vows revenge if she prove fickle. His declaration is interesting because it demonstrates that perhaps *he* is the fickle one—as evidenced by his willingness to seek revenge by transferring his affections to another woman. If his love were genuine, transference would not be so likely.

Glossary

"Hic ibat Simois; hic est Sigeia tellus; / Hic steterat Priami regia celsa senis" (28–29)   "Here flowed the river Simois; here is the Sigeian land; here stood the lofty palace of old Priam" (Ovid).

conster (30)   construe.

Pedascule (49)   a word of contempt coined by Hortensio based on the Latin "pedasculus," or "little pedant."

Aeacides (51)   descendant of Aeacus, King of Aegina and grandfather of Ajax.

gamut (66)   any complete musical scale, especially the major scale.

nice (79)   ignorant; foolish.

stale (89)   decoy, bait.

Act III
Scene 2

Summary

The wedding day arrives, and everyone is in place—except for Petruchio. As the wedding party waits for the tardy groom, they become more and more uneasy. Katherine, believing she is being stood up at the altar, refuses to be humiliated publicly and leaves. Biondello approaches and announces Petruchio is on his way, dressed in worn, mismatched clothes and riding an old, diseased horse. Grumio travels with him in much the same attire. When Petruchio arrives, he insists he will not change to more appropriate clothing. Kate, he reasons, will be married to him, not his clothes. The principals go to the church, while Lucentio and Tranio remain behind, discussing their need for someone willing to assume the role of Vincentio, Lucentio's father, and confirm the availability of the riches Tranio has promised Baptista in order to win Bianca.

Gremio enters with news of the commotion at the church. The wedding has taken place, but not without a struggle (complete with Petruchio striking the priest). At the wedding reception, Petruchio declares the wedding feast shall take place but without the bride and groom. Kate, furious, demands they stay, but Petruchio will not hear of it. He will leave, he says, and he will take all of his possessions with him—Kate included. The couple leaves, and the remaining wedding guests marvel at what they have just witnessed.

Commentary

Marriage ceremonies generally mark the end of Shakespearean comedy—but in this case the ceremony is only the beginning! In Act III, Scene 2, roughly the play's mid-point, Shakespeare gives us one of the most unusual (and unpleasant) weddings in literary history.

As the scene opens, all the preparations have been made, the guests have arrived, and Baptista and his household are ready for the ceremony to take place. The only thing missing, however, is the groom. Right away we know that something unusual is about to happen. We know

Petruchio is eager to wed and make his fortune, so it does not follow that he would not show for the wedding (particularly since the banns, the public proclamation of intent, had been read, in effect announcing the marriage contract). For him to back out at this point would bring great public shame, as well as a more immediate loss of riches.

Both Katherine and Baptista are painfully aware of the repercussions for Petruchio's breaking of the banns. Baptista declares it will be a "mockery" (4) if Petruchio doesn't show. Kate sees things even more clearly and worries about what effect being left at the altar would have on her. In fact, she trivializes her father's apparent fear of public humiliation, declaring it shall be "No shame but mine" (8). She reasons that not only is she being cornered into marriage against her heart, but she is being forced to marry an indecisive, cowardly madman in addition.

Interestingly it is Tranio who comes to Petruchio's defense, declaring he knows the man well and is sure he will arrive shortly. Tranio's response is curious on two accounts. First, Tranio appears in this scene as Baptista's right hand man and advisor. The audience is in on the joke, of course, that the man providing council is, in fact, a servant. So much for Baptista's socially discriminating judgment. On another level, Tranio's response is curious because he and Petruchio have had only minimal contact with each other (in Act I, Scene 2 and Act II, Scene 1). In fact, Tranio knows Petruchio no better than Baptista himself. In addition, Tranio and Petruchio's brief contact could not allow Tranio to judge Petruchio's character as well as he suggests. His line is, in fact, just another of his many fabrications—and why not? It is entirely in Tranio's best interest (and therefore Lucentio's best interest) to see Katherine married. His remark, then, becomes a way to buy time for the intended groom.

Character Insight

The groom does, indeed, arrive, but before he even reaches the church, people are talking about him. There is no denying Petruchio knows what is considered proper behavior for a wedding—especially his own—yet he purposely flouts convention at every turn. He is savvy enough to realize the distinction between how one acts in private and how one acts in public, as well as what is appropriate for a gentleman and what is appropriate for a beggar. Much to his credit, though, he purposely upends all custom. His purpose, of course, is to dish up to Katherine exactly what she has been serving to those around her. Part of her headstrong behavior is really a lack of understanding (or an unwillingness to understand) the rules and regulations which regulate society. She is unable to see from anyone's perspective other than her own and, in so doing, seriously handicaps her ability to impact the world around her in any way other than the most juvenile. Petruchio's lateness, his completely inappropriate dress, his disease ridden horse, his attack on the priest, and his insistence at leaving his own wedding feast are all carefully calculated measures meant to signal that his reign has begun.

Part of Petruchio's plan for besting Kate rests on providing her with a mirror image of herself in order that she may recognize her own infantile behavior. He works hard in this scene (and the next) to disorientate his bride and wear down her resistance. He deliberately enacts egregiously inappropriate public behavior, such as leaving the wedding feast, likely hoping that Kate will not miss the message he is sending her. While she may miss a more subtle text, his overt, outlandish, and inappropriate action will, in time, show Kate the error of her own actions. As if to say "See how ridiculously demanding your own way can be?" Petruchio places his own reputation on the line, temporarily (at least he hopes temporarily) acting outrageously in order to drive home a point.

As we move out of Act III, Scene 2, it is important to remember that in the time of Shakespeare, marriage ceremonies had three parts: the reading of the banns, the ceremony proper, and the consummation. Until all three parts had been completed, the marriage was considered incomplete. Here, it would be reasonable to infer the banns have been read from the few passing comments; in addition, the priest's willingness to conduct the ceremony suggests, with some degree of certainty, that the banns have been read. However, reading the banns (contractualizing the marriage to the public) and conducting the ceremony (validating the contract in front of God) comprise only two-thirds of the wedding. Until the consummation, the marriage isn't considered complete.

Glossary

rudesby (10)   unmannered fellow.

"fortune stays him from his word" (23)   "misfortune keeps him from fulfilling his promise."

turned (44)   turned inside out in order to get more wear from the material.

candle-cases (45)   discarded boots, used only as a receptacle for candle ends.

chapeless (47)   without the chape, the metal plate or mounting on a scabbard, especially that which covers the point.

hipped (48)   wounded in the hip.

glanders (50)**, chine** (50)**, lampass** (51)**, spavins** (52)**, fives** (53)**, staggers** (54)   diseases that afflict horses.

windgalls (52)   soft swellings of the fetlock joint of a horse.

yellows (53)   jaundice.

bots (54)   the larvas of the botfly.

near-legged (55)   with knock-kneed forelegs.

half-cheeked bit (56)   one in which the bridle is attached halfway up the cheek, thus not giving the rider sufficient control over the horse.

crupper (60)   a padded leather strap passed around the base of a horse's tail and attached to the saddle or harness to keep it from moving forward.

kersey boot-hose (65)   coarse, lightweight woolen cloth for wearing under boots.

list (67)   a strip of cloth.

prodigy (96)   an extraordinary happening, though to presage good or evil fortune.

"steal our marriage" (140)   "elope."

"took him such a cuff" (163)   "gave him such a blow."

list (165)   choose.

forwhy (167)   because.

rout (181)   a group of people; company (ie: a wedding party).

jolly (213)   arrogant; overbearing.

"stay my leisure" (217)   "wait until I'm ready."

action (234)   legal action by which one seeks to have a wrong put right; lawsuit.

"wants no junkets" (248)   "lacks no sweetmeats."

Act IV
Scene 1

Summary

The action switches to Petruchio's country house as the newlyweds approach. Grumio goes ahead to build a fire and, upon his arrival, tells Curtis, another of Petruchio's servants, of the adventures the couple has had while en route. Kate and Petruchio have been fighting the entire way, Grumio recounts. At one point, Katherine's horse stumbles and falls. She is thrown, and the horse lands on her. Petruchio, rather than assisting his bride, goes to Grumio and begins to beat him because Kate's horse stumbled. Katherine, covered in mud and mire, pulls Petruchio off Grumio, and the two begin to fight in earnest, scaring even the horses so much that they run away.

When Kate and Petruchio arrive, the servants line up to greet them. Petruchio wastes no opportunity to rant and rave at his serving men. The couple proceeds to dinner. As Kate's washes, a serving man accidentally spills water and in return receives a sound beating from Petruchio. Kate, in the servant's defense, claims it was an accident. When the long-awaited dinner is presented to the couple, Petruchio finds fault with it, begins a tirade, and throws the food at the servants. A hungry Kate declares "the meat was well" (157). Petruchio retorts the meat was burnt and therefore bad for their health. An evening's fast will serve them much better, and so they head to the bedchamber where Petruchio continues to censure his new bride. Returning to the stage, Petruchio explains his plan: to keep Kate hungry and uncomfortable until he successfully tames her wild behavior.

Commentary

Theme

Act IV, Scene 1, when coupled with the wedding scene just prior, gives modern audiences a rather negative view of Petruchio. Elizabethan playgoers, on the other hand, would have had very little problem with the tactics Petruchio takes to tame his wife (and they are, in fact, tactics, rather than a reflection of his true self). For Elizabethans, few problems were worse than an unruly wife. A woman dominating a man was considered an affront to his masculinity, and therefore men were encouraged to keep women in tow by whatever means possible. Men, in fact, were sometimes punished for having an adulterous wife, for instance. As if her infidelity were not enough, the husband (or cuckold) would often be subjected to additional public humiliation for allowing his wife to be out of control.

Although Petruchio's tactics seem strong to our modern sensibilities, they are nowhere near as forceful and unpleasant as some of the sermons and stories of Shakespeare's day suggest. *The Taming of the Shrew*, based in part on *A Merry Jest of a Shrew and Curst Wife, Lapped in Morel's Skin*, thankfully does not employ the same sort of punishment recommended in *A Merry Jest* (where the wife is tamed by being whipped bloody with switches and then wrapped in the freshly salted skin of Morel, the plowhorse). (See the Critical Essay section for more on this and other sources.)

In keeping with the farcical tradition in which *The Taming of the Shrew* belongs, Shakespeare fills Act IV, Scene 1 with Petruchio's comic taming tactics. We can only laugh as Grumio recounts how Kate's horse slipped in the mud, throwing her and, to make matters worse, landing on her. Petruchio, with a touch of reverse psychology, berates Grumio for letting Kate's horse slip rather than helping Kate. Later, he sends back her much-anticipated dinner, claiming it was burned and therefore would be bad for her (by producing choler, the humor supposed to bring about ill temper. She has enough of that already, reasons Petruchio). Again, he couches his remarks, appearing to be acting in her best interest. We later learn his plan is to continue to deprive her of food, rest, and other necessities, hoping to bring her to the breaking point. He admits, too, "That all is done in reverent care of her" (192) and that he'll "curb her mad and headstrong humor" by killing her with (supposed) kindness (196–197).

Character Insight

Although Petruchio appears domineering and belligerent, we quickly see he is merely assuming a role. We know from our initial contact with Petruchio that he is a clever and generally good-spirited fellow whose greatest fault may be that he is out to win his fortune. What fortune can be made, we must ask ourselves, if his wife is brutally abused and tormented throughout their marriage? Very little can come from a long-term plan for abuse. We must suspect that he is, rather, assuming a role (the tamer) until the desired goal (Kate's taming) is achieved. Petruchio's final speech in this scene, in fact, confirms that is his plan. He assumes the role of tamer, treating Kate just as she has been treating those around her. He has "politicly begun [his] reign" (176), but we must wonder whether he will, in fact, be successful. In some regards, he seems to be gaining the upper hand, treating his wife no better than an animal, but by this point we know Kate well enough not to underestimate her.

Shakespeare, in fact, continues to build our sympathy for Kate the Curst. The tacit endearment which began in earnest in Act III, Scene 2 (Kate's disastrous wedding) continues in this scene. Much of the action is highly comic, but underneath it all remains a woman who is taken out of the only environment she has ever known and placed in an entirely foreign surrounding, married to a man who equates her in every way with his other worldly possessions. Baptista, although he may have favored Bianca, certainly never treated Katherine as she is now being treated. We cannot help but feel some emotion for a woman who is forced to endure humiliation and discomfort at her husband's hands. Of course, we may reason, as Petruchio does, that she deserves no special considerations because her behavior doesn't warrant it.

Character Insight

Throughout all the commotion of Act IV, Scene 1, we can begin to see a glimmer of change in Katherine. She is beginning to mature and see the world from a perspective other than her own. Our first indication of her growth comes from Grumio's account of the journey. After her horse slipped and Petruchio began to beat Grumio for the horse's fall, Kate, seeing the foolhardy injustice of Petruchio's action, comes to Grumio's defense, wading "through the dirt to pluck [Petruchio] off [Grumio]" (69–70). Later, when one of the servants is excessively punished for spilling water as Kate washes for dinner, she is quick to come to the man's defense, claiming "'twas a fault unwilling" (144). Clearly she is beginning, ever so slowly, to see the world differently than she did in the opening acts of the play. Although it is satisfying to see Katherine mature somewhat, her change leads us to raise one of the more perplexing questions surrounding this play: Did she have to change? Critics are divided on this issue and, unfortunately, the answer becomes less and less clear as the play continues (this issue will be taken up more fully in Act IV, Scenes 3 and 5, and in Act V, Scene 2).

Glossary

rayed (3)   dirtied.

coney-catching (38)   cheating, trickery.

fustian (42)   a coarse cloth of cotton and linen.

jacks (43)   servingmen; also, drinking vessels.

jills (44)   maidservants; also "gills," drinking vessels.

fallen out (48)   quarreling.

imprimis (59)   in the first place.

foul (60)   muddy.

miry (67)   full of, or having the nature of, mire; swampy.

bemoiled (67)   dirtied with mire.

countenance (89)   to give support or sanction to; approve or tolerate.

credit (94)   pay respects to.

cock's passion (107)   by God's (Christ's) suffering.

drudge (117)   a person who does hard, menial, or tedious work.

unpinked (121)   lacking in eyelets or in ornamental tracing in the leather.

link (122)   a torch made of tow and pitch.

soud (130)   a nonsense expression of impatience.

unwilling (144)   unintentional.

dresser (151)   the person who dresses or prepares the food.

trenchers (153)   wooden boards or platters on which to carve or serve meat.

jolt-heads (154)   blockheads.

sermon of continency (171)   lecture on self-restraint; moderation.

"man my haggard" (181)   "tame my wild [female] hawk."

kites (183)   any of various accipitrine birds with long, pointed wings and, usually, a forked tail: they prey especially on insects, reptiles, and small mammals.

hurly (191)   uproar; turmoil.

humor (197)   disposition or temperament.

Act IV
Scene 2

Summary

Hortensio, angered by what he has learned of Bianca's behavior, attempts to sour Lucentio (Tranio) against Bianca. Tranio feigns indignation at the situation, appearing unwilling to believe Bianca would love anyone but him. Before long, Tranio must admit Bianca exhibits more than a passing interest in Cambio (the real Lucentio). Hortensio, increasingly enraged, vows he will foreswear Bianca and gets Tranio to agree to reject her as well. Hortensio continues, pledging to marry a wealthy widow "Ere three days pass," resolving "Kindness in women, not their beauteous looks, / Shall win my love" (41–42).

Lucentio, Bianca, and Tranio are overjoyed to hear Hortensio has abandoned his pursuit of Bianca. As they discuss their good fortune, Biondello enters with news: An old man approaches. Lucentio and Tranio are still looking for an old man to assume the role of Lucentio's father (so the imposter-father can vouch for the financial solvency of imposter-Lucentio). Tranio, still masquerading as Lucentio, convinces the old man, a Mantuan schoolteacher, that his life is in peril if he is found in Padua (because of a supposed war between the Duke of Padua and the Duke of Mantua). Tranio tells the old man that he may disguise himself as Vincentio of Pisa and thereby avoid risking his life. In return, the old man need only confirm the dower he offered Baptista for marrying Bianca.

Commentary

Act IV, Scene 2 returns us to Padua and the play's subplot. The scene, generally comic in nature, accomplishes two major things. First, it removes Hortensio from the love triangle and helps set up the marriage triad which is so crucial to Act V, Scene 2. Next, Lucentio and Tranio find an old man to impersonate Lucentio's father, Vincentio, and make the last part of their charade complete.

Theme

Hortensio's quick and simple rejection of his beloved Bianca may strike us as curious, but his action contributes to Shakespeare's predominate themes of courtship and marriage. Hortensio is easily as fickle as any woman in his feelings for Bianca. Instead of gracefully removing himself from the love triangle, Hortensio removes himself with an unwarranted vengeance (which, rest assured, will later earn him what he deserves). He is quick to curse Bianca, but the joke really is on him, as the audience is well aware. Hortensio's somewhat cryptic line "Would all the world but he had quite forsworn!" (35) provides a clue as to his folly. He says, in essence, that he hopes everyone in the world will forsake Bianca except the poverty-stricken Cambio, leaving her with what she deserves—nothing. In reality, though, Cambio is far from poor and is, in fact, quite a good catch.

Theme

Through Hortensio's easy transference of affection, from Bianca to the unnamed widow, Shakespeare again directs our attention to the fleeting nature of supposed "love." As we have seen before, marriage is, for Hortensio as well as other male characters, merely a business transaction. Hortensio feels pressure to be married, so he shall be. He admits to selecting a potential spouse based on beauty (41), but when that doesn't work, he opts for selecting one based on "kindness" (41). We will see later, though, that Hortensio did not necessarily follow his own advice, opting instead to marry for financial reasons (not unlike his good friend Petruchio).

Perhaps the character who comes off best in this scene is Tranio. We see he is as clever and capable as his master—perhaps even more so. He is able to think on his feet easily and has no problem playing Hortensio like a lute. The only place where Tranio's behavior makes audiences take pause is when he claims Hortensio has "gone unto the taming-school," however (55). He could have had no indication such was the case unless Hortensio delivered the information off stage or in now lost lines.

In addition to easily mastering Hortensio, Tranio succinctly maneuvers the Pedant into precisely the position he desires. Unlike Tranio, the Pedant is a flat, rather gullible character. He is quickly taken in by Tranio's fiction and, in fact, considers himself lucky to have found such a benefactor. Ironically, the Pedant is quite the opposite from Vincentio, the man he will impersonate. Biondello, in fact, says as much, when he mutters the two men are as like "as an apple doth an oyster" (102–103). Humorously, the poor unknowing Pedant will impersonate one of the richest and most well known men in Pisa while he, himself, is of much a much meaner background. Instead of riches, he delivers "bills for money by exchange" (90), or promissory notes.

Glossary

profit (6) reap an advantage or benefit.

resolve (7) determine; answer.

The Art of Love (8) Ovid's *Ars Amatoria.*

proceeders (11) workers.

despiteful (14) spiteful; malicious.

wonderful (15) that causes wonder; amazing.

cullion (20) a low, contemptible fellow.

lightness (24) wantonness.

fondly (31) foolishly.

haggard (39) a wild hawk.

"eleven-and-twenty long" (58) "right on the money"; allusion to the card game "one-and-thirty."

marcantant (64) a merchant.

pedant (64) a schoolmaster.

"let me alone" (72) "count on me."

stayed (84) stopped; halted.

credit (108) the favorable estimate of a person's character; reputation; good name.

"take upon you" (110) play your part.

repute (114) regard.

pass assurance (119) to give a legal guarantee.

dower (119) that part of a man's property which his widow inherits for life.

Act IV
Scene 3

Summary

The third scene of Act VI opens on Kate and Grumio at Petruchio's house. A very hungry and sleep-deprived Kate attempts to convince Grumio to bring her some nourishment. Not unlike Petruchio, Grumio taunts Kate with thoughts of food, only to claim he cannot produce any food because "'tis choleric" and therefore not good for her. In exasperation, Kate orders Grumio away after having given him a beating for tormenting her so. Petruchio and Hortensio enter, and Petruchio offers Kate some food. Until she thanks him for providing it, however, she cannot have it. Reluctantly she gives in and receives her meal.

Petruchio announces they will return to Baptista's house, dressed in the finest clothes money can by. As if to prove his intention, Petruchio calls forth a tailor with a gown and a haberdasher with a hat, both for Kate. He proceeds to berate the haberdasher's work, turning a deaf ear to his wife's declaration that the hat is perfect. After berating the work of the haberdasher, Petruchio turns to the work of the tailor, finding countless faults with the dress. In the end, the tailor is sent away with the gown (although Petruchio slyly makes arrangements to pay for the goods, unbeknownst to his wife). Petruchio turns to Kate, claiming they'll just travel in the clothes they have "For 'tis the mind that makes the body rich," not the clothes (168). He announces that it is currently 7 a.m. so they should be to Minola's around noon. Kate corrects him, stating it is almost 2 p.m. and they won't arrive until suppertime. Petruchio rants that the trip is off because his wife can't agree with what he says, and until she learns to do so, the awaited trip home is postponed.

Commentary

This scene returns us to Petruchio's house and to a Kate who is beginning to break down under Petruchio's tactics. It's important to note, though, she still retains her edge. As the scene opens, we are greeted by a ravenous Kate desperately trying to get Grumio to bring her some food. Be sure, too, that although she is hungry, she is not starving. She has not been endangered or abused, but merely kept hungry and awake for a little while. How can we be sure? She has power and strength enough to beat Grumio when he plays his malicious game of food-naming with her (a game in which he obviously delights). If Petruchio were abusing her, she would not be capable of the sorts of things she does in this scene. We must smile, in fact, at Kate's declaration she is

Starved for meat, giddy for lack of sleep,
With oaths kept waking, and with brawling fed.
And that which spites me more than all these wants,
He does it under name of perfect love,
As who should say, if I should sleep or eat
'Twere deadly sickness or else present death.
— (IV.3, 9–14)

Clearly Petruchio's claim that he deprives Katherine of meat and sleep because of his deep love for her is even making her think he's a bit mad. She is, of course, being treated with the same selfish, childish behavior she herself has precipitated for years—only Petruchio is, if possible, even a bit more outlandish because his treatment comes under the guise of caring too much as opposed to not enough. Again, it would not seem that Kate could miss the mirror being held up to her.

We see Kate in the process of changing in this scene, but her change is only the most superficial. When Petruchio brings her some food but is not thanked properly, he threatens to take it away. Kate realizes that, in order to get her meal, she will need to thank her provider because, as Petruchio notes, "The poorest service is repaid with thanks, / And so shall mine before you touch the meat" (45–46). At this point Kate offers "I thank you, sir" (47) but surly a less heartfelt offering of thanks could not be uttered. Although Kate is learning some of the rules of the game, she has a long way to go.

Petruchio's declaration of a visit to Baptista's house immediately sets off alarms in the audience. It is seemingly out of character with the antics Petruchio has been orchestrating, especially when he announces they will "revel it as bravely as the best / With silken coats and caps and golden rings, / With ruffs, and cuffs, and farthingales, and things" (54–56). As suspected, Petruchio is using the situation as a teaching lesson. Should Kate understand the game at this point and behave in the manner he seeks, there is no doubt Petruchio would set out for Padua immediately. He knows his wife, however, and is quite certain of her headstrong ways. He is clever, too, in the tools he chooses for this lesson. Rather than food or sleep, essentials to every human, he opts to use luxuries to gain leverage. First, a trip to Padua is exactly what Kate wants. It gets her back to a place with which she is familiar and where she is accustomed to getting her own way. Petruchio combines that motivation with lovely clothes, appealing to her vanity, for extra punch.

Character Insight

We know even more clearly by this point that Petruchio is genuinely good natured and is putting on a show for Kate. His hyperbolic ranting and raving at the haberdasher and the tailor is merely a spectacle to show Kate how ridiculous her own behavior has been. Notice how Petruchio is sure to draw Hortensio aside at line 159 and arrange for him to pay the tailor for his services. (Whether Petruchio expects Hortensio to pay for the work out of his own money is unclear, however. If he does, Hortensio's willingness to do so speaks loudly of Petruchio's ability to sway not just women, but men too.)

Throughout the action of this scene, Hortensio remains a curious fellow. He has arrived at Petruchio's house en route to his widow. In one sense, he seems to provide a sort of validation to the scene. With Hortensio present, we can be assured Kate will not be maltreated. He provides a somewhat neutralizing effect to Petruchio's ravings. He also provides side commentary to the action. He comes across as a nervous fellow who can hardly believe what he's seeing before him (a role he'll pick up again in Act IV, Scene 5). He also serves as an opposite to Petruchio. The two men are completely different, of course, but Hortensio is so flat and dull that Petruchio looks all the better.

As the scene draws to a close, it is time for another lesson. It is after noon, yet Petruchio insists it is seven in the morning and so they will arrive at Minola's house around noon. Kate, knowing the day is over half gone, notes it is almost two in the afternoon, placing their arrival at supper, rather than the noon dinner. Her correction is most valid and not necessarily ill intended. It is merely a statement of fact. However, Petruchio uses the occasion to rail yet again, chastising Katherine that no matter "what I speak, or do, or think to do, / You are still crossing it . . . . / I will not go today, and ere I do, / It shall be what o'clock I say it is" (188–191). Kate is a very clever woman, and there can be little doubt that she is beginning to understand what her husband is up to. Hortensio, though, has seen the whole exchange and clearly has no idea of what's unfolding before him; he ends the scene incredulously marveling at how Petruchio thinks he will command the sun. Little does Hortensio realize just how likely that is!

Glossary

neat's foot (17)   foot of a bovine animal (ox, cow, etc.).

amort (36)   dejected, disspirited.

"sorted to no proof" (43)   "proved to be to no purpose."

bravely (54)   splendidly dressed.

bravery (57)   finery.

porringer (64)   a bowl for porridge.

cockle (66)   cockleshell.

trick (67)   trifle.

custard-coffin (82)   pastry crust for a custard.

demicannon (88)   large cannon.

censer (91)   an ornamented container in which incense is burned.

braved (109)   defied.

quantity (110)   fragment.

be-mete (111)   measure; thrash.

"think on prating" (112)   "remember this thrashing."

bottom (133)   ball or skein.

trunk (137)   full; wide.

"for thee straight" (147)   ready for you immediately.

mete yard (148)   measuring stick; yardstick.

odds (150)   inequalities.

furniture (176)   furnishings, clothes.

Act IV
Scene 4

Summary

Tranio, disguised as Lucentio, and the Pedant, disguised as Lucentio's father Vincentio, have come to see Baptista Minola about the dower. When the Pedant speaks with Baptista, he eloquently confirms the dower's availability. Tranio, delighted the plan is working so well, quickly suggests all parties involved draw up the binding agreements straightway. Tranio also suggests sending Cambio to tell Bianca the news. Cambio re-enters as the stage clears, and Biondello informs him of Tranio's plan to arrange a fake wedding so Lucentio can marry Bianca himself for real. In light of this new arrangement, Cambio hurries off to inform Bianca they are to be wed that very night.

Commentary

As with other small scenes of the subplot, this one contains little action but does advance the play in a few crucial ways. First it helps to indicate the passing of time, a necessity if we are to believe the action of the primary plot. Further, we need to see the importance of the disguised father so that we can be prepared for the play's resolution.

This scene also reinforces how much marriage is a matter of economics. Baptista has, in effect, sold his youngest and most beloved daughter to the highest bidder. The joke is on him, of course, since in being so concerned with money he has been duped by a servant and an old man who haven't much money between the two of them together. In Baptista's greed, he seems to have worked his daughter right out of a suitable husband (whether that's true or not will be resolved in Act V). All Tranio had to do was give the appearance of being a gentleman, and he was afforded every advantage a gentleman should have, even beating out the competition by invention of a make-believe fortune.

Likewise, the Pedant's ability successfully to fool Baptista projects interesting light on the socially accepted concept that people of rank were distinguished by their birth. As we see in Shakespeare, time and time again, such is not always the case. Shakespeare, in fact, often uses his disguises to show the foolishness of the nobility who insist on taking people at face value and who are certain gentlefolk are different from commoners. As we see here, given the proper disguise, landed gentry have a hard time discerning who is authentic and who is an imposter.

In addition, Tranio's presence in the scene reinforces the economic side of marriage. When Baptista is quick to agree to put the marital negotiations in writing (thereby making them binding), he shows his primary concern is a legal one. In fact, Baptista's preoccupation places him in an almost pathetic light. When he innocently offers comments such as sending Cambio to tell Bianca "how she's like to be Lucentio's wife" (66), we cannot help but laugh at his foolishness. Bianca, of course, will become Lucentio's wife—but not in the way Baptista thinks.

Glossary

"hold your own" (6) "play your part."

right (12) genuine, real.

tall (17) fine.

"set your countenance" (18) "put on the expression of an austere father."

"with one consent" (35) unanimously.

curious (36) unnecessarily inquisitive; prying.

lie (56) lodge.

pass (57) transact.

slender pittance (61) scanty banquet.

counterfeit assurance (92) pretend wedding.

"cum privilegio ad imprimendum solum" "with exclusive printing rights."

"against you come" (103) "in anticipation of your arrival."

roundly (107) vigorously, bluntly, severely, etc.

Act IV
Scene 5

Summary

Petruchio, Kate, and Hortensio are on their way to Baptista Minola's house in Padua. It is midday, yet Petruchio notes the moon shines brightly. When Kate contests his claim, insisting it is the sun which shines, Petruchio threatens to force the party to return to his home, insisting "It shall be moon, or star, or what I list / Or ere I journey to your father's house —" (7–8). At this point, Katherine begins truly to understand the elaborate game Petruchio is playing. She learns that if she humors him, she will get something she wants, and so she agrees with whatever Petruchio says. Kate's willingness to compromise is quickly put to the test when old Vincentio, father to Lucentio, meets the travelers. Petruchio, as if testing his wife, asks her whether she has ever seen a "fresher gentlewoman." Kate, aware she is being tested, plays Petruchio's game with good-natured zeal, no matter how many times Petruchio changes his mind.

Once the couple is through playing their game, Petruchio gets Vincentio to explain what brings him toward Padua. Vincentio notes that he is on his way to visit his son. Petruchio, now assuming the dignity and kindness which befits a man of his status, notes that Lucentio has married his wife's sister. He speaks well of Bianca but leaves Vincentio marveling at what he's just heard. Despite their earlier joking, Petruchio insists he speaks the truth. The party moves on, leaving Hortensio behind to marvel at the change he has just witnessed in Katherine. He ends the scene by suggesting that he will follow Petruchio's lead and tame his widow, if need be.

Commentary

Character Insight

Although Act IV, Scene 5 is the shortest scene of the play, it is clearly the most important one so far. Here we see Kate coming to understand that, when she agrees to let Petruchio have his way, she reaps the benefits. It is not at all certain that Kate is *tamed* by her husband; rather through the situations he involves her in, she *develops*, moving from a selfish girl lashing out in defense against her father's favoritism, to a more mature woman who finally sees adult life is made of compromises.

Many critics see Act IV, Scene 5 as marking the point of Kate's defeat. In reality, she is not defeated at all. The game which she has played expertly up until the time of her marriage (getting her way through ranting and bullying) has changed and become far more sophisticated. Rather than succumbing to Petruchio's demands, she learns that marriage is built around give and take; it is a compromise. When she chooses to follow the rules, she is rewarded—and so is Petruchio. By humoring Petruchio in his purposely outlandish demands that the sun is the moon, the moon is the sun, and that the old man a young woman, Kate's life runs much more smoothly.

Petruchio, on the other hand, will gladly give Kate anything she desires, as long as she is willing to humor him. In some senses, perhaps, this game gives Petruchio power, but it is power he is willing to share with her. He, too, is glad to compromise once the initial rules are met. Further, he knows Kate has come to understand what he's up to; her good humored and elaborate replies clearly reveal she is willing to play his game and perhaps best him at it, too. Petruchio knows he has an especially wise wife who can match his wit and will if she so desires. In the end, Kate has not lost anything. Rather, a new world has opened to her—an adult world with adult compromises and consequences. Her increased maturity is, in fact, quite becoming.

Literary Device

Vincentio's arrival on the scene moves us toward the play's inevitable intertwining of the primary and secondary plots. With all the disguising which has occurred in the play, Vincentio's arrival isn't totally unexpected. As with all good comedies of mistaken identity, an outsider (or person innocent of the disguising which has taken place) is needed to reveal the masquerade and set the action toward the path of resolution. Interestingly, Vincentio is momentarily taken aback by the travelers' news, however, since they strike him more as a team of practical jokers than a powerful husband lording over his submissive wife (a distinction that we must remember as we head toward the play's denouement).

Finally, this scene, like the third scene in Act IV, makes a point of including Hortensio. There is, of course, no likely reason he would need to journey to Petruchio's house prior to wedding his widow, but his appearance here has two distinct effects. First, when Kate and Petruchio call Vincentio a "fair lovely maid" (33) and "Young, budding virgin, fair, and fresh, and sweet" (36) Hortensio frets "'A will make the man mad, to make a woman of him." (35). The couple, though, continues in jest, signaling Hortensio is an outsider to their game. He worries about Vincentio taking offense, whereas Petruchio and Kate are caught up in their own world and are unconcerned with upsetting the old man. In short, through Hortensio's offhand remark, Shakespeare shows us how in this scene Petruchio and Kate come together as a team.

Hortensio, through his comment at scene's end, also helps us see that Petruchio is admired for his accomplishment. Hortensio marvels: "Well, Petruchio, this has put me in heart. / Have to my widow! And if she be froward, / Then hast thou taught Hortensio to be untoward" (76–78). He is clearly impressed by Petruchio's ability to enact such a change in Katherine. He has come to realize that the feat which he thought impossible at the end of Act IV, Scene 3 has come to pass; Petruchio *is* able to command the sun. In keeping with his shallow nature, however, Hortensio recognizes little about what has unfolded before him. All he knows is that he wants to emulate Petruchio so as to get his wife to follow him as well as Kate follows Petruchio. Little does he realize that being "untoward" (78), or unmannerly, is only part of the trick. A firm foundation in sincere affection, as we shall see in Act V, is crucial as well.

Glossary

list (7)   wish.

or ere (8)   before.

"Where away?" (27)   "Where are you going?"

green (46)   fresh; new.

"by this" (62)   "by this time."

esteem (63)   favorable opinion; high regard; respect.

beseem (65)   to be suitable or appropriate.

"break a jest" (71)   "play a joke."

jealous (75)   very watchful or careful in guarding or keeping.

"put me in heart" (76)   "encouraged me."

Act V
Scene 1

Summary

Lucentio (no longer disguised as Cambio) and Bianca head to the church to be married while her father is busy making arrangements with Tranio and the Pedant. Petruchio, Kate, Vincentio, and Grumio arrive in Padua and stop at Lucentio's house. Vincentio insists his companions join him for a drink, but upon knocking at the door and announcing himself, he is surprised to find another man who claims to be Lucentio's father. When Biondello appears, Vincentio questions him. Biondello pretends not to recognize his master's father. When Tranio comes to investigate the commotion, he too pretends not to know Vincentio. When the Pedant defends Tranio, claiming he's Lucentio, Vincentio moans that Tranio must have murdered the real Lucentio and assumed his persona. Baptista, unwilling to put up with such wild behavior, orders Vincentio to prison. At this point the newlyweds, Lucentio and Bianca, return.

Lucentio explains what has happened, why Tranio was masquerading as his master, and announces his marriage to Bianca. Baptista and Vincentio reconcile minimally and enter the house to untangle the situation in which they find themselves. Gremio, realizing he has no hope for a spouse, goes inside to join the wedding feast. Petruchio asks Kate for a kiss, and when she refuses, he threatens to return home again. Good humoredly, she kisses her husband before heading in to the feast.

Commentary

Finally, in Act V, Scene 1, we arrive at the long awaited discovery scene. As wise connoisseurs of drama, we've known from the beginning that the disguising must be unraveled, and so it is, and in fine comic fashion. Of course, in keeping with comic tradition, little punishment is doled out, although Vincentio's feathers are certainly ruffled. After all, what gentleman wants to find out that not only has his identity been successfully stolen, but stolen by someone of a lower class, at that!

Vincentio's arrival marks a return of order to the play. He is an outside force who is sober in judgment. Innocent of what has transpired in Padua since his son's arrival (and used to being treated as his high rank would dictate), he is unprepared for what he finds upon reaching Lucentio's house and has no reason not to be outraged. The Pedant has successfully assumed Vincentio's identity—so fully, in fact, that he feels comfortable in disparaging the real Vincentio's wife, offering a backhanded slur about her reputation, stating Tranio is really Lucentio "so his mother says, if I may believe her" (33).

Of course before the mistaken identities can be sorted out, confusion must reach its apex, and it does so with Biondello and then Tranio refusing to acknowledge they know Vincentio. What they're doing, in part, is attempting to buy time for their master, Lucentio, who has not yet returned from his secret marriage to Bianca. When Lucentio finally returns (line 101), Tranio, Biondello, and the Pedant all retreat "as fast as may be" (s.d. 105), glad to extract themselves from a situation in which they were not likely to fare well.

Baptista's and Vincentio's anger seems to be diffused upon the announcement that Lucentio and Bianca are married. Their response is, of course, the appropriate response given this is a comedy. In keeping with comic tradition, Shakespeare necessarily moves toward positive resolution and re-establishment of the proper social order, and how else could he do that, in this case, but have the two fathers pass over the wrongs done to them and celebrate their children's marriage. Note, however, that as the two patriarchs leave for the feast, Vincentio comments he will "be revenged for this villainy" (128) while Baptista vows "to sound the depth of this knavery" (129). Shakespeare is careful to keep all retribution off stage, as he does in all his comedies, so we are not distracted by punishment, but rather, invigorated by the successful marriages.

Character Insight

As the scene ends, all but Petruchio and Kate have gone inside to the wedding feast. The last few lines are very telling and solidify the change in the couple (not just Kate) brought about in the prior scene. Kate begins their exchange this time, suggesting "Husband, let's follow, to see the end of this ado" (134). Surely she is not powerless since she is capable of suggesting the route of action they, as a couple, should take. Petruchio agrees to her suggestion, but desires a kiss first. Up until this point, we have seen no such display of affection, and Kate's initial refusal, we learn, is not because she doesn't want to kiss him, but that she doesn't want to kiss him *in public*. She relents and gives Petruchio a kiss, but again, it is under subtle threat (more comic than real, this time) of having to return home and miss the feast. Petruchio, himself, seems genuinely pleased at the situation, wondering "Is not this well?" (142). The scene closes with Petruchio addressing his bride as "my sweet Kate" (142), a phrase which here assumes genuine sincerity as opposed to the ironic terms of endearment uttered in Act II. Just as much as Katherine has changed, so too has Petruchio. It seems the two have truly come to love each other.

Glossary

father's (9)   father-in-law's.

"You shall not choose but drink" (11)   "I insist that you drink."

flat (35)   absolute; positive.

cozen (38)   to cheat; defraud.

good shipping (40)   bon voyage.

crackhemp (43)   rogue likely to end up being hanged.

offer (59)   dare.

copintank (62)   high-crowned, sugar-loaf shape.

"good husband" (63)   "good provider."

'cerns (70)   concerns.

maintain (71)   afford.

coney-catched (93)   tricked.

"wert best" (98)   "might as well."

haled (101)   pulled forcibly; dragged; hauled.

counterfeit supposes (110)   suppositions; false appearances.

packing (111)   conspiracy.

"My cake is dough" (132)   "I'm out of luck."

"Out of hope of all but" (133)   "Having no hope except."

Act V
Scene 2

Summary

In this final scene, all the characters come together to celebrate Bianca and Lucentio's wedding. Hortensio has arrived with his new wife, the Widow, and the three couples begin to converse. Petruchio notes how Hortensio appears to be afraid of his wife, with the Widow offering a few particularly nasty retorts. Kate and the Widow exchange words, and shortly thereafter the three women exit, leaving the men to their devices.

The men decide to wager on who has the most obedient wife. They bet one hundred crowns and one by one send for their wives. Lucentio is immediately refused by Bianca. Hortensio is next to be refused, with his wife adding the command he should come to her. Finally Petruchio takes his turn, and all are surprised when Kate comes to do his bidding. Petruchio sends Kate to fetch the other women and, upon their arrival, tells Kate to destroy the hat she wears (which she does) and then lecture the women on "What duty they do owe their lords and husbands" (135). After Kate delivers an elaborate speech about a woman's duty to her husband, the party-goers are left dumbfounded, and Petruchio and Kate leave the party, headed to bed.

Commentary

Some critics regard this scene as one of the more enigmatic in Shakespearean comedy, but such a claim is really unwarranted. Oftentimes people are surprised at Kate's speech (some even claim it sours an otherwise good play), but upon closer inspection it appears clear that her speech is in no way a concession; rather, it carries a much stronger message and brings the play to a clever resolution. Shakespeare gives us ample suggestions that audiences should not take Kate's soliloquy at face value but instead should look beyond the literal to the deeper meaning this passage contains.

One of the first clues that Shakespeare intends Kate's speech not be taken literally is that the soliloquy comes in the context of an entertainment. Although Kate appears to speak earnestly, we must remember that she is playing a role in a game. The notion of husbands betting on their wives, in fact, is laughable and adds an air of merriment to the feast.

After the women leave, the men are left to their devices. Petruchio clearly stands above all the other men in that he is gracious and dignified, offering a toast not only to the health of the newlyweds, but also "all that shot and missed" (51). The general consensus among the men, however, is that Petruchio has fared the worst of all, ending up with the woman Baptista himself calls "the veriest shrew of all" (64). Knowing the joke will be on the men, Petruchio calls for a wager. He even demands the ante be increased to an amount worthy of his wife. His willingness to wager on Kate is not mercenary or dehumanizing, as some critics might think, but rather, is a testament to his faith in her. He is, in essence, trusting her with his reputation. He's not the sort of man who would enter a contest so boldly if he weren't sure of winning. He is confident in his ability to understand Katherine, and she does not let him down.

Lucentio begins the contest by summoning Bianca. Although just hours earlier she was demure and willing to do his bidding, Bianca is now headstrong. Her denial of Lucentio, in fact, serves as a hint of what's to come. Bianca, who's name means "white" and is associated with purity, is not at all pure of spirit. In fact, she has been disguised all along and after catching her husband, she is quick to abandon her false front.

Hortensio takes up the challenge next, and after Bianca's refusal to appear, we are not at all surprised to find the Widow will not come when beckoned. In fact, the Widow insists "She will not come. She bids you come to her" (96). The Widow is no fool and is unwilling to give up even an ounce of her power. Why did she marry Hortensio, then? Most likely because of economic reasons. The tide is turned on Hortensio who thought *he* was gaining economic independence (plus revenge on Bianca) by marrying the Widow.

All eyes are on Petruchio when he calls his wife. He commands her presence (as opposed to Lucentio's bidding (79) and Hortensio's entreating (90)), and much to everyone's surprise she appears. At this point, the crowd is flabbergasted, and their surprise provides Kate and Petruchio just the opportunity to get the best of all of them. Kate is aware

Petruchio is not only staking his reputation on her, but he is giving her the opportunity to have power over all others present. By asking Kate to go get the other women, Petruchio gives her an opportunity to lord over the others. Later, in getting her to stomp on her hat, the couple works together to give the *illusion* of Petruchio having control, while in reality, they share power together and reap the mutual rewards (remember, what is real and what is illusory is a large theme in this play and must not be forgotten in the end).

Kate's soliloquy on wifely obedience is, perhaps, the most important of the play. Throughout the play, Shakespeare has been careful to poke fun at the institution of marriage and here is no exception. Also, we know from the other comedies that Shakespeare is particularly empathetic to female characters. A truly anti-feminist reading would be unlikely, given what we know of other Shakespearean heroines. Further, this is the longest speech of the play—Shakespeare wouldn't give Kate the final word unless we were to feel affection for her—something that is not possible if you read her as being defeated and broken. Finally, facility with language is considered a masculine trait, and for Kate to exhibit such linguistic aptitude suggests that she has not totally abandoned her masculine ways.

Style & Language

Exploring the language of Katherine's soliloquy shows, too, that she is having fun. Many of her expressions are hyperbolic, not unlike much of the rhetoric Petruchio used earlier on her. She repeats the sentiment of the time—a sentiment she knows will please the ears of her listeners (thereby giving her an advantage as well as an opportunity to get whatever she desires). She does make an interesting distinction, though, between obeying one's husband blindly and obeying with discretion. She claims that one should be "obedient to his honest will" (162), which has the implication that, when the husband's will is *not* honest, his will is not to be obeyed, an important distinction when considering whether Kate has been truly "tamed."

After Kate finishes her speech, Petruchio asks again for a kiss, and this time Kate gladly complies. Petruchio then suggests they head off to bed, with the obvious implication of consummating their marriage, thereby making it official. Kate is glad to agree, and so the two exit together. All the others are left to ponder what they have just seen, while we can likely reason that Kate and Petruchio will live happily ever after, working together to dupe and gull the world around them, two players in a game only they understand.

Glossary

scapes (3) escapes.

respecting (32) compared to.

"Ha'to thee" (37) "Here's to thee."

butt (39) to strike or bump against; to bump with the head.

"Have at you for" (45) "Be on guard against."

health (51) a wish for a person's health and happiness, as in drinking a toast.

slipped (52) unleashed.

gird (58) gibe; scoff; jeer.

galled (60) injured or made sore by rubbing; chaffed

sadness (63) seriousness.

"I'll be your half" (81) "I'll cover half your bet (for half the winnings)."

"by my halidom" (103) "by my holiness."

swinge (108) to punish with blows; beat; whip.

aweful rule (113) authority commanding awe or respect.

pass (128) state of affairs.

"Confounds thy frame" (144) "Ruins your reputation."

watch (154) spend or pass.

simple (165) having or showing little sense or reasoning ability.

"Unapt to" (170) "Unfit for."

big (174) boastful; pompous; extravagant.

"vail your stomachs" (180) "lower your pride."

boot (180) profit, use.

"go thy ways" (185) "well done."

toward (186) obedient.

sped (189) done for.

CHARACTER ANALYSES

The following character analyses delve into the physical, emotional, and psychological traits of the literary work's major characters so that you might better understand what motivates these characters. The writer of this study guide provides this scholarship as an educational tool by which you may compare your own interpretations of the characters. Before reading the character analyses that follow, consider first writing your own short essays on the characters as an exercise by which you can test your understanding of the original literary work. Then, compare your essays to those that follow, noting discrepancies between the two. If your essays appear lacking, that might indicate that you need to re-read the original literary work or re-familiarize yourself with the major characters.

Katherine Minola

Like many other of Shakespeare's comedies, *The Taming of the Shrew* features a woman as one of the story's chief protagonists. Katherine Minola is a fiery, spirited woman, and as such, the male dominated world around her doesn't quite know what to do with her.

Much of what we know about Kate initially comes from what other people say about her. In Act I, for instance, we see her only briefly and hear her speak even less, yet our view of Katherine is fairly well established. Shakespeare, though, is setting up a clever teaching lesson, helping us later to see the errors of our own hasty judgment (just as characters in *Shrew* will also learn lessons about rushing to judgments). Right after Baptista announces that Kate must marry before Bianca may take suitors, Gremio colors our interpretation of the elder daughter by declaring "She's too rough for me" (1.1.55). Later in the scene, Gremio reiterates his dislike for Kate, demeaning her as a "fiend of hell" (88) and offering that "though her father be very rich, any man is so very a fool to be married to hell" (124–126). He finishes off with the declaration that to marry Kate is worse than to "take her dowry with this condition: to be whipped at the high cross every morning" (132–134). Hortensio, too, is quick to add to the foray, calling Kate a devil (66) and claiming that she is not likely to get a husband unless she is "of gentler, milder mold" (60). Tranio, Lucentio's servant, is perhaps the only man in this scene not to disparage Kate, diagnosing her as "stark mad or wonderful froward" (69).

Kate, in her own defense, offers telling commentary on her situation. Although other characters encourage us to see her as unmannerly and incorrigible, deserving of marginalization and abuse, looking more closely at what Kate actually says reveals she may not be as domineering as some characters would have us believe. For instance, the first lines we hear her speak are to her father, imploring him not to wed her to a fool (57–58). Although it is somewhat nervy for her to speak out against her father, the fact that she does so in order to make what seems to us to be a fairly reasonable demand helps us see her as reasonable rather than shrewish.

In Act II, we get another look at Katherine and learn a bit more about what motivates her seemingly outrageous behavior: She's responding to the favoritism she perceives Baptista holds toward her sister, Bianca. As Act II opens, Kate enters, dragging Bianca with her hands tied. On one level, the mere act of one sister roping the other and handling her roughly for a perceived injustice is comic, but when we stop and consider from Kate's perspective we can have a bit more empathy. Kate is venting her anger that Bianca should be indulged with suitors while she remains alone. Granted, she is an intelligent and spirited woman who wouldn't be satisfied with simpering men such as Gremio and Hortensio. Rather, she needs a strong man to compliment her own strong and powerful personality. When Baptista enters and comes to Bianca's rescue, we learn what's really underlying Kate's behavior: She's angry at the way Baptista favors her younger sister. She confronts her father, claiming Bianca is his "treasure" and "must have a husband" while she, humiliated, dances "barefoot on her wedding day" and leads "apes in hell" (II.1, 31–36).

Although Katherine, in the early acts of the play, seems reasonably well motivated in her actions, the manner in which she carries out her feelings is perhaps what most marks her as a shrew. Her actions are decidedly unladylike, revealing Kate's inability to deal in an adult manner with what she is feeling. In short, she comes across as a child who has learned that the best way to get what she wants is to cajole, bully, and lash out, whereas later she will reason and be able to contain her behavior. From early on, we see Kate is a scrapper, ready to enter into a physical brawl rather than risk not getting her way. No matter how justly motivated we may find her actions, the fact she is quick to lash out signals an immature approach to life.

By the time the play hits its midpoint, however, Kate begins her transformation, moving from egocentric misery to a decidedly more mature happiness found, in this case, through marriage. We see the beginning of Kate's change on the ride to Petruchio's house after the wedding. In Act IV, Scene 1, Grumio travels ahead of his master and mistress in order to prepare for their welcome. He recounts the horrors of their travels, including Katherine's slipping off her horse and the horse landing on her (64–75). Petruchio's response was to beat Grumio for letting the horse stumble. Kate, it would seem, would use this occasion to enter into a grand fight, but rather, she waded through the mire to pull Petruchio off Grumio. This simple act of defense signals that Kate is, in fact, capable of considering a perspective other than her own. Shortly after arriving at the house, Kate again shows her kindness in defending a servant who has accidentally spilled some water (141–145).

Kate's character continues to be revealed as the play progresses. As the couple travels back to old Baptista's house, for example, she begins to see how Petruchio's partnership works. She quickly learns that, if she gives in to what Petruchio says, even if she knows it to be false, she'll get something she wants (for example, they'll travel to her father's house). The test, of course, comes when they meet the real Vincentio on the road, and Petruchio questions Kate as to whether she has ever seen a finer young woman. Rather than arguing the contrary, Kate shows her incredible wit by not only agreeing with him, but also good-naturedly adding to the game! At this point, she has clearly come to understand that Petruchio has a method to his madness, and she begins to realize their relationship can be a partnership with a series of actions and rewards.

Perhaps in no place is Kate seen as more enigmatic than in her final speech. Although some readers' initial impulse is to take the ending at face value, the speech, like Kate herself, is far more rich and dynamic than that. Underlying the speech is Kate's awareness that she is in a partnership and that by advancing the power of her husband she advances her own power. In addition, she is clearly aware of the distinction between public and private behavior, and there is no indication that her assuming this temporary and very public role of suppliant means she will always be that way—especially in private. It shows, also, that Kate has come to a level of maturity, able to handle things in an adult manner (in which there is both give and take). Kate's speech does not reflect a tamed shrew, but rather a richer, more developed woman than the one seen at the story's beginning.

Petruchio

Although Kate is one of Shakespeare's most enigmatic heroines, she is not the only complicated character in *The Taming of the Shrew*. Her groom, Petruchio, has nearly as much mystery surrounding him as does Kate herself. Yet exploring Petruchio forces us to ask questions that can become difficult largely because, frankly, we want to like him. In a sense, it's initially hard to explore a side of him which may, in fact, make him less likable. Is he a man of honor or a mercenary seeking only to marry into money? Is he domineering and truly worthy of the title "tamer," or does the role he takes with Katherine constitute something less aggressive and ultimately more democratic? To be sure, in the end, it's clear Petruchio is not nearly as mercenary as we might initially think. In fact, when all is said and done, Petruchio is a successful match for the strong-willed and ebullient Kate.

The first difficult issue we must deal with if we are to look at Petruchio fairly is his early claim that he has "come to wive it wealthily in

Padua; / If wealthily then happily in Padua" (I.2, 74–75). Certainly this doesn't sound like a declaration from a man destined to marry for love. Rather, it sounds like a man who is following the common, traditional pattern for the time: making the best alliance he can for himself, elevating his status as much as possible through marriage. If we accept that Petruchio does indeed want to marry solely for financial gain, then another line of questioning arises: If all he wants is money, once he has Katherine's hand (and dowry), why then does he try to help her (and himself) to a better life? It would have been far simpler to treat her poorly, as most shrews in the literature of the time were treated.

It seems as if Petruchio surprises even himself when he realizes that although he outwardly wishes to marry for money, when it comes to it, he is motivated by something else: the desire to love and be loved. Petruchio, rather than being domineering and selfish, is an observant man who quickly senses in Katherine something more than her outward shrewishness. He sees beyond the superficial (unlike Lucentio who falls in love with Bianca based on what he has observed) and aptly recognizes that her behavior is a masquerade, a tough exterior intended to cover her inner desire to be loved and valued. On top of that, Petruchio becomes so attracted to her spirit and her non-conventional nature that when he accomplishes his initial desire to "wive it wealthily," he takes his involvement a step further, making a great effort to help Kate develop, sensing that the true Kate, when she can be brought out, will compliment him well.

Part of what makes Petruchio so likeable is his apparent disregard for social decorum, particularly when he works to get Kate to abandon her shrewish exterior. For instance, he doesn't buy into the notion of "birthright," as we see by his refusal to treat Katherine as a woman of her status traditionally expects to be treated. Rather, Petruchio's treatment of Kate is based on how she behaves. She has to earn her privileges. We see another good example of Petruchio's willingness to go against convention in an ends-justifying-the-means fashion when he arrives late for the wedding. To be sure, though, it is this exact willingness to go against convention that keeps Petruchio from being a paragon for the Elizabethan man (remember, class and social stratifications were encouraged by those in power during Shakespeare's time). Many of the ordinary people who initially viewed the plays (they made up the bulk of the audience) would likely have seen Petruchio as a hero, but to those in power, aspects of Petruchio's behavior would have been cause for concern.

Another aspect of Petruchio's nature that adds to his appeal is the way in which he grows to trust his wife—something none of the other characters do. The play's final scene provides the best example when, in the midst of the banquet, Petruchio eagerly puts his reputation in Kate's hands. For him, the initial twenty crown wager is an insult, causing him to exclaim "I'll venture so much of my hawk or hound, / But twenty times so much upon my wife" (V.2, 73–74). Kate comes when she is called, as Petruchio was sure she would, but in giving Kate the task of telling "these headstrong women / What duty they do owe their lords and husbands" (V.2, 144–145), he releases complete control of his reputation. At this point, whatever she says will reflect not only on her, but on him as well. At this point Petruchio is also giving Kate an unparalleled opportunity: to address and instruct the party. Clearly he trusts her—so much, in fact, that he is willing to share the public forum with her (an extraordinary occurrence for a woman). Kate's formidable speech leaves her own husband speechless, able to exclaim only "Why, there's a wench!" (184).

Although in many ways Petruchio is like his wife, admittedly he doesn't undergo the same sort of maturation and development as she does (after all, his tyranny is clearly a fiction, a parody created to help Kate see the senselessness of her behavior). It would be unfair, though, to claim he remains static. When we look back to the Petruchio of the early acts, he is determined to live solely for himself, intending to exist largely on the dowry of the wife he hopes to find. If this were his sole motivation, though, what point would there be in his taking the time to help his wife into a partnership? If money were his only goal, surely he wouldn't bother trying to help Kate to a different perspective. When it comes to it, it seems Petruchio does not, in fact, want merely to wive it wealthily. He wants someone who can spar wits with him, challenge him, and excite him intellectually, emotionally, and physically. By the wedding scene, Petruchio has come to this realization; hence, he willingly assumes the all-important role as the catalyst for Kate's change. For instance, purposely arriving late, wearing conspicuously inappropriate attire, and behaving in a completely improper manner at the wedding mark Petruchio's initial steps in getting a wife worth more than merely her money. By play's end his gamble to try and bring Kate to a higher level of understanding pays off. Petruchio gets the mate he desires—but he, too, is changed. He is no longer the mercenary man from the early acts; rather he is a man deserving of the extraordinary partner he has gained.

CRITICAL ESSAYS

On the pages that follow, the writer of this study guide provides critical scholarship on various aspects of Shakespeare's *The Taming of the Shrew*. These interpretive essays are intended solely to enhance your understanding of the original literary work; they are supplemental materials and are not to replace your reading of *The Taming of the Shrew*. When you're finished reading *The Taming of the Shrew*, and prior to your reading this study guide's critical essays, consider making a bulleted list of what you think are the most important themes and symbols. Write a short paragraph under each bullet explaining *why* you think that theme or symbol is important; include at least one short quote from the original literary work that supports your contention. Then, test your list and reasons against those found in the following essays. Do you include themes and symbols that the study guide author doesn't? If so, this self test might indicate that you are well on your way to understanding original literary work. But if not, perhaps you will need to re-read *The Taming of the Shrew*.

Of Shrews and Shrew Tamers: Shakespeare's Historical Basis for *The Taming of the Shrew*

The Taming of the Shrew, popularly regarded as rather sophisticated for such an early Shakespearean comedy, joins the rest of the works in the Shakespeare canon in its ability to extend its roots back to early sources. In addition to being linked to a specific source or two, though, *Shrew* is linked, as well, to literature, ballads, and courtesy books that council how to deal with a shrewish woman. Although today *The Taming of the Shrew* might seem chauvinistic to us because it celebrates the merits of male power and dominance, we must consider it within its historical context in order to distill the most meaning from the play. When we look at *The Taming of the Shrew* in this light, we see the main action of the play takes its cue from a long tradition of works dealing with shrews and shrew tamers. It would be a gross error to say, though, that Shakespeare wholeheartedly endorses complete male rule. Although *Shrew* does extol some of the common stereotypes of the shrewish woman (and her subsequent need for reformation), it also begins to challenge the common folklore, providing spectators with something familiar which also advances a more non-traditional theme when it comes to dealing with an unruly wife.

During the Renaissance, the controversy over women took various forms, sometimes debating their basic nature, their legal and moral rights, their clothing, and their behavior. The branch of the debate most central to *The Taming of the Shrew*, though, centers on appropriate and inappropriate female behavior (shrewishness and scolding), particularly within the confines of a marriage wherein the husband was traditionally viewed as the ultimate authority figure.

A Merry Jest of a Shrewd and Curst Wife Lapped in Morel's Skin, for Her Good Behavior, a popular and fairly lengthy ballad composed around 1550, is commonly regarded as one of the primary works in the public debate regarding the appropriate treatment for unruly women in Renaissance England. Although this work was printed only once and very few copies remain, Shakespeare would have undoubtedly been familiar with this ballad since its popularity led to the story circulating orally as an elaborate folktale.

In *A Merry Jest*, two sisters figure prominently, the younger of which is favored by the girls' father and sought after by gentlemen callers while the older sister is shrewish and headstrong. The ballad proceeds much like Shakespeare's *Shrew*, with the curst daughter marrying a man who spends the rest of the ballad trying to break his wife of her headstrong ways and bring her into line with societal expectations. In the end, though, Shakespeare's *Shrew* ends nothing like the ballad wherein the wife's husband plots to break his wife by beating her and then wrapping her in the freshly salted hide of a horse (formerly) named Morel. Predictably, the wife repents after this treatment (which, admittedly most Elizabethans would not have seen as unusually cruel) and lives the rest of her life peaceably, serving and obeying her husband.

Just as Shakespeare found precedent for his discussion of shrewish women, so too did he find precedent in ways to deal with them. Where there are shrews, of course, there must be shrew tamers—and it is in this regard that Shakespeare is perhaps his most tacitly crafty. Whereas Kate fits quite well within the traditional paradigm of the shrewish woman (being bold, aggressive, talkative, and physical), Petruchio does not so readily fit the stereotype of the shrew tamer. His actions reflect a degree of restraint and understanding not commonly seen in other shrew-tamers of the period. The husband in *A Merry Jest of a Shrewd and Curst Wife*, for example, sees nothing at all wrong with beating his wife bloody and then wrapping her in a salted horse's hide until she repents her shrewish and headstrong ways. He believes it is his right as her husband, a notion which the wife's family is quick to corroborate. No punishment, however painful and seemingly unjust (by modern standards, anyway), is too harsh for a shrewish wife. Petruchio, though, doesn't resort to such means. He is clever, and it is that cleverness that allows him to reform his wife without ever laying a hand on her. He keeps her awake and denies her a bit of food, but these punishments are small compared to the punishments routinely doled out in the literature and stories of the time.

It is important to note, too, that the Elizabethans clearly delineated between a "shrew" and a "scold." A shrew, although a pejorative and abusive term, had no real legal status. A scold, on the other hand, is a legal category and describes a woman who has offended against public order through her speech. Unlike the shrew whose unruly behaviors are mostly disorderly and aggressive, a scold routinely committed more slanderous acts. Tale-bearing, gossiping, slandering, insulting through speech, and deliberately and maliciously attempting to stir up trouble between neighbors were all actions that could bring legal punishment onto a scold. If a woman were to be punished for such behavior, she would receive a public "cucking" wherein she was strapped to a special stool and then repeatedly dunked into water. Other forms of punishing scolds existed as well, most of which allowed for community participation. Scolds (and occasionally their husbands who allowed them to get away with it) were commonly held in great contempt by their neighboring townsmen and often received public punishment including humiliation in the stocks or being paraded through the city on a leash wearing a scold's bridle (a contraption which fit over a woman's head and contained a metal tongue suppressor to prohibit her speaking) so people could come out and jeer (hopefully shaming the transgressing woman back into line with what was considered proper womanly behavior).

The manner in which Shakespeare has Petruchio tame Kate, though, is not nearly as aggressive (or dangerous) as the methods that were actually used. Petruchio stands out positively, in fact, as being able to manifest the change in Katherine because of his cleverness and his rhetoric rather than brute force and beating. In this regard, Petruchio is much more in line with William Gouge and William Whately, who both received a great deal of pressure for advocating male restraint when dealing with unruly wives. Domestic violence at this time was commonplace, and wives were rarely exempt from forcible correction. As one critic notes, "relatively few men or women in early modern England thought wives had an absolute right not to be beaten" (Hunt qtd. in Dolan 218). Clearly Shakespeare does not endorse this model because in the end Kate and Petruchio function as a team rather than as a master and a servant.

Certainly it is possible to view Petruchio as a tamer, a man out to turn a headstrong woman into a subservient one, but his role goes beyond that. Unlike most men of his time, he seeks not to dominate, but to share his power with his wife. Would he ever have been attracted to a woman such as Bianca whom he could easily rule? Of course not, because he needs someone to match his own fiery nature. Interestingly, the other male characters, though, see only that Petruchio has succeeded in turning the most headstrong of women into a seemingly perfect wife. Hortensio (and Christopher Sly in the variant text, *The Taming of A Shrew*) sees Petruchio has enacted a metamorphosis in Kate, unaware of the cleverness and rhetorical strategy underlying his techniques. Hortensio (Sly, and presumably many of the men in the audience) thinks he will emulate Petruchio's behavior. However, without the necessary cleverness, tenderness, and motivation (to elevate rather than subjugate), Hortensio will never succeed.

Shakespeare creates wonderful characters in *The Taming of the Shrew*, wonderful in part because they are not constructed solely from his imagination. They come from a long tradition of stories and ballads on unruly women and the men who try to tame them. Some contemporary readers may view *Shrew* as a misogynistic work, but it really is much more. It is a work based in historical debate and, in fact, ends more positively than many of its literary and real-life counterparts. Through Petruchio, especially, Shakespeare advocates a world in which men try not to exercise absolute authority over their wives but, rather, to elevate their wives. Shakespeare's text, unlike so many of the historical counterparts, suggests that successful men and women work in tandem rather than in hierarchal fashion, and so doing elevates not only the husband and the wife, but by extension, everyone and everything they come into contact with, as well.

Lights, Curtain, Action!: Role Playing in *The Taming of the Shrew*

"You are come to me in happy time, / . . . for I have some sport in hand / Wherein your cunning can assist me much" says the Lord to the players in the Induction of *The Taming of the Shrew*. These seemingly simple words of welcome resonate, setting the context for the story about to unfold before us. We know that theatricality will be paramount to the story as the clever Induction pulls us into the drama through the story of Christopher Sly's duping. The Induction focuses our attention on the idea of appearances being deceiving, as well as on the importance of acting and role playing, but then it stops abruptly once *The Taming of the Shrew* proper begins. Why then take the time to introduce us to Sly and the merry jest of the Lord and his household? We can see the Induction as functioning in a number of ways (see the Induction commentary for more), but one of its most important purposes is to clue spectators into one of the play's main themes: role playing. In *Shrew*, Shakespeare provides disguises of all shapes and forms, from obvious physical disguises to more subtle psychological ones, and in the confines of a play within a play allows us to see a world which, not unlike our own, is teeming with role players.

The first and most obvious type of disguise employed in *Shrew* is the physical disguise. The notion of physical role playing is introduced at the very beginning of the play and continues throughout. When Christopher Sly falls asleep, the Lord decides to play a trick on him by having him carried to his manor and dressed as a nobleman. Lucentio, in Act I, Scene 1, assumes the role of Cambio, Bianca's tutor, while his servant, Tranio, disguises himself as Lucentio. Later, at the end of Act II, Scene 1, Tranio/Lucentio realizes he will need to present Vincentio, Lucentio's father, so he decides "suppos'd Lucentio/ Must get a father, call'd suppos'd Vincentio" (II.1, 407–408), and in Act IV, Scene 2, he finds a Pedant to play the part (72–121). We are introduced to yet another masquerader in Act III when Hortensio disguises himself as Litio, Bianca's music tutor. Aside from proper clothing, the only other thing these role players seem to need in order to ensure their masquerades is someone to corroborate their stories. Certainly the ease with which these players enact their roles suggests that as spectators (both inside and outside the theater) we need to be aware that nothing is as it seems and that we are continually surrounded by people who may just be acting a part in order to obtain a desired outcome.

A bit less obvious than the physical disguises are the psychological disguises in *The Taming of the Shrew*. Both Kate and Petruchio assume psychological disguises. Kate becomes a shrew to compensate for the hurt she feels because of her father's favoritism toward Bianca. In addition, she refuses to be saddled with an unworthy husband and so assumes the role of a shrew, insulating herself from the hurtful world around her, no matter how much she may secretly wish to join in the fun. Likewise, Petruchio assumes the role of shrew-tamer, exaggerating Kate's bad behavior until she cannot help but see how infantile and childish her actions have been.

Bianca, too, assumes a psychological disguise, changing her perspectives drastically once she is safely married. Although she appears initially as a demure and pure soul, by play's end we see that is not the case. As the play draws to a close, we see more and more of Bianca's true disposition and learn that, ironically, it is Bianca, not Kate, who really is the shrew! In her case, her psychological disguise provided her the opportunity to appear better than she really was, suggesting again that we must be wary of the role playing going on around us. Physical disguises are fairly easy to detect and defuse, but psychological disguises are quite a different and more complicated matter.

Psychological and physical disguises, though, aren't the only ways to look at the role playing in *The Taming of the Shrew*. The play is also, in many respects, self-reflective. It is metadramatic in the sense that it is self-reflexive, calling attention to the fact it is a play and the actors are all taking a part. Use of metadramatic devices is not unique to *Shrew*, however. Shakespeare often uses these devices in his plays to offer spectators inside jokes about the players, the drama, or the men playing the roles, as well as to draw attention to the artificiality of what we see before us and to urge us to recognize the elements of drama that permeate our daily lives. For instance, in *Shrew*, the Induction provides a framework for the obvious performance we are about to witness. There must be no mistake about it: What we are about to see is not a mirror held up to life; rather, it is a fiction created by a troupe of actors (note, too, how calling attention to the play as a fiction rather than a slice-of-life lessens the seriousness of the play's message of male authority).

Besides the Induction and the obvious physical disguises (costumes, if you will), we can also see Shakespeare calling attention to his play as just that, a play, through the characters of Kate and Petruchio. Rather than seeing them as the shrew and the tamer, we can also see them as analogous to an actor and a director. In very literal terms, the character of Kate is created by a young man playing a woman who creates a shrewish persona for herself so she can more easily deal with the world around her (largely through avoiding it). When her disguise is no longer useful to her (or when the director, Petruchio, has finally convinced her to abandon the disguise) she assumes another role—this time the dutiful wife (thinking of Kate as an actress also helps with interpreting her speech in Act V, Scene 2).

Petruchio is the director who orchestrates the production we see before us. He theorizes on how to get Kate to do what he wishes and begins planning his performance early. Although the staging of Petruchio's performance starts at the wedding when he assumes the costume of a wild man, he stages his largest production when he vows to kill his wife with kindness. In helping Katherine to a more mature state of being, Petruchio dictates all the particulars, just as a director dictates a production. He runs the show, so to speak, governing when his wife will enter and exit, when she will eat and sleep, when the action will advance and when it will repeat itself, and even attempts to oversee time itself. He very carefully sets up the elaborate production at hand, helping move his shrewish wife into desirable mate.

Disguising and role playing of all sorts fill the scenes of *The Taming of the Shrew*. In addition to advancing the general plot, the pervasive disguising and metadramatic nature of the play suggest that role players abound and that, as wary spectators, we must be like Petruchio, careful not to take things at face value because we are surrounded by duplicitousness.

CliffsNotes Review

Use this CliffsNotes Review to test your understanding of the original text and reinforce what you've learned in this book. After you work through the review and essay questions, identify the quote section, and the fun and useful practice projects, you're well on your way to understanding a comprehensive and meaningful interpretation of *The Taming of the Shrew.*

Q&A

1. *The Taming of the Shrew* was written

   a. early 1590s

   b. late 1590s

   c. after 1605

2. In the Induction, Sly is convinced he is a gentleman by being told

   a. he's just inherited a great deal of money

   b. he married a wife with a great deal of money

   c. he's been ill which made him *think* he was a beggar

3. Which of the following men are in love with Bianca?

   a. Lucentio, Hortensio, Grumio

   b. Lucentio, Hortensio, Gremio

   c. Lucentio, Tranio, Hortensio

4. From the time Petruchio meets Baptista Minola until the day of the wedding is

   a. about 3 weeks

   b. about 3 months

   c. about a week

5. Which of the following statements is *not* correct?

   a. Hortensio is from Padua

   b. Petruchio is from Rome

   c. Lucentio is from Florence

Answers: (1) a. (2) c. (3) b (4) c. (5) b.

Identify the Quote: Find Each Quote in *The Taming of the Shrew*

1. Am I a lord? And have I such a lady?
Or do I dream? Or have I dreamed till now?
I do not sleep: I see, I hear, I speak,
I smell sweet savors, and I feel soft things.

(Induction.2, 68–71)

2. Tranio, I saw her coral lips to move
And with her breath she did perfume the air.
Sacred and sweet was all I saw in her.

(I.1, 75–77)

3. I come to wive it wealthily in Padua;
If wealthily, then happily in Padua.

(I.2, 74–75)

4. 'Tis bargained twixt us twain, being alone,
That she shall still be curst in company.
I tell you, 'tis incredible to believe
How much she loves me. O, the kindest Kate!
She hung about my neck, and kiss on kiss
She vied so fast, protesting oath on oath,
That in a twink she won me to her love.

(II.1, 302–308)

5. I am to get a man—whate'er he be
It skills not much, we'll fit him to our turn—
And he shall be Vincentio of Pisa
And make assurance here in Padua
Of greater sums than I have promised.

(III.2, 131–135).

6. . . . amid this hurly I intend
That all is done in reverent care of her.
And in conclusion she shall watch all night,
And if she chance to nod I'll rail and brawl,
And with the clamor keep her still awake.
This is a way to kill a wife with kindness;
And thus I'll curb her mad and headstrong humor.

(IV.1, 191–197)

7. See how they kiss and court! Signor Lucentio,
Here is my hand, and here I firmly vow
Never to woo her more, but do forswear her,
As one unworthy all the former favors
That I have fondly flattered her withal.

(IV.2, 27–31)

8. Young budding virgin, fair, and fresh, and sweet,
Whither away, or where is thy abode?
Happy the parents of so fair a child!
Happier the man whom favorable stars7
Allots thee for his lovely bedfellow!

(IV.5, 36–40)

Answers: (1) [Christopher Sly, upon waking at the Lord's house, attempts to makes sense of the situation in which he finds himself.] (2) [Lucentio speaking of Bianca. He has just seen her and, in perfect courtly love fashion, has fallen immediately in love with her.]. (3) [Petruchio's original explanation on what brings him to Padua.] (4) [Petruchio, trying to save face with his peers after his first encounter with a very feisty, angry, and unreceptive Kate.] (5) [Tranio explaining how he and Lucentio will pull off their masquerade and get someone to verify the existence of the riches Tranio (disguised as Lucentio) has offered in his quest for Bianca.] (6) [Petruchio, now married, explaining how he has "politicly begun [his] reign" (4.1.176) and how he will break his wife of her bad behavior without seeming to cast himself in a negative light.] (7) [Hortensio to Tranio/Lucentio, rebuking his affection for Bianca. Apparently his love is as fickle as hers.] (8)[Katherine addressing Vincentio, an old man. This passage signals that Kate has finally come to understand the game Petruchio is playing and is, in fact, willing to play along with him.]

Essay Questions

1. What purpose does the Induction and the story of Christopher Sly serve?

2. Compare and contrast the two Minola sisters, both at the beginning and the end of the play. What do you learn?

3. Trace the disguises assumed in *The Taming of the Shrew*. What makes each disguise more or less successful than another? What might Shakespeare be trying to say?

4. Examine Kate's final speech on marital duty carefully. What evidence can you fine (in that speech or elsewhere in the play) that she is delivering this passage seriously? On the other hand, what suggests that she may not believe her own words completely?

5. Shakespeare places the theme of love (platonic, romantic, and filial) at the forefront of this drama. Based on your reading, how are each of these forms of love characterized? What do you think Shakespeare is saying about the nature of each?

Practice Projects

1. Take on the persona of one of the play's characters. Demonstrate your understanding of the text by writing a letter of introduction (from a paragraph to several pages) from the perspective of your character. What motivates you? What do you value? What can't you stand? What questions would you ask the other characters if given the chance?

2. Compare the text of *Taming of the Shrew* to a classic production (such as the Elizabeth Taylor/Richard Burton version) or a modern adaptation (*Ten Things I Hate About You*). How do these productions stack up against the original? What parts do they represent faithfully and what sentiments do they change or eliminate entirely?

3. Using a search engine, do a search for Web sites related to *The Taming of the Shrew*. Assemble a list of sites, critically annotating each one with a few sentences (not just summarizing its content, but really considering the credibility of each site). Pool your findings with some of your peer's to create a thorough list of resources available.

CliffsNotes Resource Center

The learning doesn't need to stop here. CliffsNotes Resource Center shows you the best of the best—links to the best information in print and online about the author and/or related works. And don't think that this is all we've prepared for you; we've put all kinds of pertinent information at www.cliffsnotes.com. Look for all the terrific resources at your favorite bookstore or local library and on the Internet. When you're online, make your first stop www.cliffsnotes.com where you'll find more incredibly useful information about *The Taming of the Shrew.*

Books

This CliffsNotes book provides a meaningful interpretation of *The Taming of the Shrew.* If you are looking for information about the author and/or related works, check out these other publications:

William Shakespeare's **The Taming of the Shrew:** *Texts and Contexts,* edited by Frances E. Dolan. Dolan has assembled an impressive array of historical documents which complement the full text (also included) nicely. This scholarly book features thoughtful commentary on Shakespeare's play, as well as the historical documents which inform our understanding of it. If you want more information on what life was really like for a shrew or a shrew tamer, this is the work for you. New York: Bedford St. Martin's, 1996.

From Farce to Metadrama, by Tori Haring-Smith. For those interested in staging plays and production history, Haring-Smith's work is for you. This work covers the chronological development of *Shrew's* staging, addressing historical variations in stage productions and shifting cultural notions about marriage. Westport, Connetticut: Greenwood Press, 1985.

Shakespeare A to Z : The Essential Reference to His Plays, His Poems, His Life and Times, and More, edited by Charles Boyce & David White. If you're looking for additional information of *The Taming of the Shrew*, Shakespeare, or essentially anything related to him or his works, this is one resource you won't want to miss. Organized like an encyclopedia, Boyce's work puts specific and well-researched topics at your fingertips. The scholarship is solid and thorough, helping make *Shakespeare A to Z* a source you'll return to again and again. New York: Delta, 1991

Shakespeare For Dummies, by John Doyle and Ray Lischner. As with all the *Dummies* guides, this work provides comprehensive information in an easy-to-follow format and does much to remove the intimidation people sometimes feel when it comes to studying Shakespeare. *Shakespeare For Dummies* will give you more information regarding *The Taming of the Shrew*, as well as all of Shakespeare's other works and the time in which he lived. The work is accessible and has something for everyone—from the first-time Shakespeare reader to the seasoned veteran. Indianapolis: Wiley Publishing, 1999.

It's easy to find books published by Wiley Publishing, Inc. You'll find them in your favorite bookstores (on the Internet and at a store near you). We also have three Web sites that you can use to read about all the books we publish:

- www.cliffsnotes.com
- www.dummies.com
- www.wiley.com

Internet

Check out these Web resources for more information about William Shakespeare and *The Taming of the Shrew*:

Mr. William Shakespeare and the Internet, daphne.palomar.edu/ shakespeare—Hands down, the most comprehensive Shakespeare Web site around. This site provides students of all ages and levels with tools to help access not only Shakespeare's texts and language, but productions, as well as ample information on his life and times. This site provides a delightful blend of academic and light-hearted information on the beloved Bard.

Surfing with the Bard, www.ulen.com/shakespeare/students/ guide—A brief guide dedicated to helping you become familiar with Shakespeare's play. This easy-to-navigate site is conveniently broken into three major areas: reading the plays, viewing the plays, and Shakespeare on the Web.

Sites on Shakespeare and the Renaissance, castle.uvic.ca/ shakespeare/Annex/ShakSites1.html—This user-friendly site is a good springboard into a host of Shakespeare-related sites. Sponsored by the University of Victoria in British Columbia, the information here goes beyond *Shrew* to cover the whole Shakespeare canon with links to criticism, graphics, sound, video, performance information, research resources, study materials, and other sites for Shakespeariana.

Next time you're on the Internet, don't forget to drop by www.cliffsnotes.com. We created an online Resource Center that you can use today, tomorrow, and beyond.

Films and Other Recordings

Check out these films for a fun look behind the scenes of a *Shrew* production and adaptations of the play itself:

Kiss Me, Petruchio, New York Shakespeare Festival Productions. Films Incorporated, 1983. A sneak peek into the *Shrew* production staged as part of the New York Shakespeare Festival. It combines snippets of performance with the principal actors discussing their roles. Meryl Streep and Raul Julia are phenomenal in this production and help us in understanding what really drives Kate and Petruchio. If you have to work a bit to find a copy of this production don't be daunted. The search will be more than worth it! Directed by Christopher Dixon.

Taming of the Shrew, RCA/Columbia Pictures Home Video, 1967. In general, Elizabeth Taylor/Richard Burton films are not to be missed—and this film is no exception. Directed by Franco Zeffirelli and produced in grand Zeffirelli style, the film is a feast for the eye and the ear. This production plays up the struggle between chauvinism and feminism and brings out the physical comedy that runs throughout *Shrew*. Although some scenes seem a bit overblown, generally the production is solid and has become the mark to which other film productions are inevitably compared.

10 Things I Hate About You, Touchstone Pictures, 1999. This witty retelling of Shakespeare's classic tale moves the action from Padua, Italy to Padua High School where the school newcomer, Cameron James (Joseph Gordon-Levitt), seeks to win the affection of Bianca (Larissa Oleynik), the girl of his dreams. The largest obstacle, though, is Bianca's father who has decided Bianca cannot date until her boy-hating sister Kat (Julia Stiles) has a boyfriend (Heath Ledger). Despite (or perhaps because of) the movie's high school setting, the film sparkles with cleverness and puts a modern spin on a timeless tale. Worth viewing simply to compare and contrast with the original text. Directed by Gil Junger.

Magazines and Journals

Following are some articles that you may find interesting in your study of Shakespeare's *The Taming of the Shrew:*

Boose, Lynda E. "Scolding Brides and Bridling Scolds: Taming the Woman's Unruly Member." *Shakespeare Quarterly.* 42 (1991): 179–213. Boose explores Shakespeare's text through the filter of historical evidence, looking especially at scolds and how they were to be dealt with. This article, although not for everyone, includes great visuals of the bridles—the monstrous and often painful contraptions to which scolds were sometimes subjected.

Dusinberre, Juliet. "*The Taming of the Shrew:* Women, Acting, and Power." *Studies in the Literary Imagination.* Spring 1993: 67–83. Like all of Dusinberre's work, this article captivates readers with the way it draws on the facts of what was, to springboard into what quite likely might have been. Here Dusinberre explores the politics of the original staging of *Shrew*, examining in detail the metadramatic nature of Shakespeare's text. Readers will gain insight into *Shrew* as well as the company which staged this drama and the community which flocked to see it.

Send Us Your Favorite Tips

In your quest for knowledge, have you ever experienced that sublime moment when you figure out a trick that saves time or trouble? Perhaps you realized you were taking ten steps to accomplish something that could have taken two. Or you found a little-known workaround that achieved great results. If you've discovered a useful resource that gave you insight into or helped you understand *The Taming of the Shrew* and you'd like to share it, the CliffsNotes staff would love to hear from you. Go to our Web site at www.cliffsnotes.com and click the Talk to Us button. If we select your tip, we may publish it as part of CliffsNotes Daily, our exciting, free e-mail newsletter. To find out more or to subscribe to a newsletter, go to www.cliffsnotes.com on the Web.

Index

NOTES